# BUSINESS COMMUNICATION
## Practical written English for the modern business world

Cynthia Beresford

BBC English by Radio & Television

# Introductory Note

This book is intended for anyone who handles business communication in English.

It can be used for self study or classroom work, either individually or in groups. It assumes a knowledge of English to at least Intermediate level.

By using a series of clear models and exercises, the book illustrates the language needed for different communicative functions. It demonstrates the use of both formal and informal register.

The models are based on authentic situations, and are followed by systematic revision and vocabulary building exercises.

# Acknowledgements

The BBC wish to thank:
Dr Butt Oswald of Carl Freudenberg GmbH, Weinheim.
Tony Harman, Fellow of the Royal Entomological Society.
William Mallinson, CBE, Vice-Chairman of Smiths Industries.
Dun & Bradstreet Ltd, London.
Rear Admiral D. W. Kirke, CB, CBE, of Airship Industries Ltd.
Students of the Institute Kreatives Lernen, Frankfurt.
Students of Alfred Teves GmbH, Frankfurt.
The staff and students of Pilgrims Language Courses Ltd, Canterbury.

Reprinted 1985, 1988, 1990, 1992
Printed by Butler & Tanner Ltd, Frome and London
Typeset by the Pitman Press, Bath

ISBN 0 946675 71 6

# CONTENTS

# How to use this book

These notes are intended for students working on their own. Teachers will find some suggestions for using the book in class just before the key.

## Before you start work

First of all, look at the Contents, familiarising yourself with the business topics covered. Then skim quickly through the entire book. You will see that each unit includes:

— Models for letters, memos, reports and other standard written forms covering a wide range of business situations. These models have often been adopted from actual documents
— Common phrases, selected to be as useful as possible in a wide range of contexts
— Exercises practising either language points or business terms.

## Working through a unit

a. Understanding the model
Before starting to write, you need to understand written business English. Look at some of the model letters. They often have questions besides them, which are intended to increase your powers of comprehension by focusing your attention on specific points. Study these questions, and try to ask similar ones when you receive letters at work. You will soon find it easier to understand both the structure and content of the letter or document. (What is its purpose? Is it a standard reply – or a letter of application?) and the implications. You will learn how to 'read between the lines'.
It is important to understand what the person writing to you *really* means. For instance, is the tone formal or informal? Recognising different degrees of formality is discussed in Unit 1. Business letters carry factual information. But they may also, like personal letters, convey information about the quality of the business

relationship between two firms. Suppose you have an old and valued customer who happened to be late with a payment. It would be wrong to write a really angry letter. Instead, you could convey your irritation more subtly by adopting a more formal tone than usual.
b. Practising the language
When you have fully understood one of the models, look at the phrases which follow it. Could you use them in letters of your own? Now turn to the exercises. They take several different forms:
— filling in blanks with appropriate phrases
— writing something similar to the model
— language practice and use of common business phrases
— précis e.g. turning a letter into a telex.
Many of the exercises have answers in the key at the back of the book.

## When you have finished

Remember to revise at regular intervals, one week and one month after finishing a unit. If you do this, you will be surprised at how much you can remember. But without revision you are likely to forget and so waste the effort you have put in. Revision need not take long, it's just a question of reminding yourself what was in the unit. However, in your initial work and your revision you will need a dictionary.

## Choosing a dictionary

A good monolingual dictionary is an essential aid to anyone studying a language. Bi-lingual dictionaries can be helpful but their use is limited. Small pocket dictionaries can actually be misleading.
When choosing a dictionary check:
– Does it contain a clear guide to how to use the dictionary?
– Does it give alternative meanings as well as the definition?

– Is an American/English equivalent given when necessary? What about American spellings?
– Is there a clear example of the word in context?
– Can you tell if the word in question is formal, informal or slang?

Recognising when to use a particular word is one of the skills practised in this book.

## Dealing with new words

When you meet a new word first of all, try to predict what it means. Look for clues. This can be done by asking yourself the following questions.

1) What is the context of the word?
2) What part of speech is it? For example, 'we can bid' (verb) or 'we can make a bid (noun) for a contract'.
3) Can you recognise and understand the root of the word?
4) What does the prefix or the suffix indicate?

Decide whether it is important to know the *exact* meaning. If it is not preventing you from understanding the gist of the text, carry on reading. Return later to the unknown word and then consult your dictionary. Note the context, the negative forms, synonyms and any interesting uses or idioms.

## How to get the most out of your dictionary

Learn to say and use the alphabet quickly. Check that you are pronouncing the letter correctly. This will help you to find words quickly. Refer to the head words in the top left and top right hand corners of each page.

It is important that you understand the meaning of the symbols, abbreviations not the different typefaces used. This is **bold**, this is *italic*.

Make a special effort to understand, recognise and practice using the phonetic and stress symbols. When you have learnt a new word, check the number of syllables and the pronunciation. Say it aloud to yourself and put it into a sentence. Note what happens to it when it is used as a noun, and when it is used as a verb. Note if the stress changes.

1) Get a supply of small cards, about the size of visiting cards.
2) When you find a new word or phrase which is important, write it in the centre of the card.
3) Write the definition in your own language on the reverse side.
4) Make personal notes on the face of the card.

Accumulate a pack of cards (hold them together with an elastic band). These can be slipped into your pocket and be referred to at odd moments of the day. As you learn each card, exchange it for a new one. This way you can build up your own personal dictionary.

In this Unit you will find:

**A.** Formal and informal letters confirming an invitation
**B.** Opening and closing phrases establishing the tone of a letter
**C.** Memos
**D.** Telexes

## A1   A formal letter confirming an invitation

Here is a formal letter from the Managing Director of an international company written to an important customer whom he has never met. Read it carefully. Use the information given in this letter to complete the informal letter which follows.

```
Dear Mr. Comelli,


     Proposed Visit - October 19th/20th

We are delighted to know that you will be in Greece on October
19th.  This is to confirm our telephone conversation.  We shall
meet you at Athens airport at 1530.  By coincidence, our
Scandinavian agent, Mrs. Larssen, is on the same flight.

We have reserved a room for you at the Grand Hotel for the 19th
and 20th.  The Heads of Department will join us for dinner which
has been arranged for 2100 on the 20th.

In view of your other commitments, we will endeavour to cover
the complete programme in one day.  Here is a suggested timetable.


     0930  Review last year's results
     1000  Evaluate new products
     1030  Determine price levels for new season
     1100  Coffee
     1115  Finalise promotional activities
     1215  Negotiate renewal of agency contract (Lunch)
     1430  Visit Quality Control laboratory to settle
           Spring Hotel's complaint (in Quality Control lab.)
     1530  Discuss long-term Research and Development
     1600  Inspect new high-speed unit

I realise it is a very full programme, but there will be an
opportunity to discuss outstanding matters in a more relaxed
atmosphere over dinner.

I look forward to meeting you on the 19th.

Yours sincerely,
```

## An informal letter

Anna Larssen is an agent who has known Mr Ioannou for many years. She is on the same flight as Mr Comelli. Fill in the gaps in the letter below. Choose from the list of words in the margin.

a. tie up (this means to finalise)
b. into
c. pick you up
d. booked  3
e. laid on  5
f. chance

> Dear Anna,
>
> We are very pleased that you will be here with us for the session on the 20th.  We can certainly .....(1)..... at the Airport at 1530.  Quite by .....(2).. our Italian agent, Antonio Comelli, of the Albani Group, will be on the same flight.  We have .....(3).. you both .....(4).. the Grand Hotel, and we have .....(5).. dinner at 2100 for nine of us on the 20th.  I know you have a tight schedule, so we will try to cover everything in the one day.  There will be time to .....(6)..... any loose ends over dinner.

## A2  Formal and informal language

Compare the informal language Mr Ioannou used in his letter to Anna Larssen with the more formal language in his letter to Mr Comelli.

'We shall meet you at the airport.'
'We can certainly pick you up at the airport.'

'By coincidence our Scandinavian agent, Mrs Larssen, is on the same flight.'
'Quite by chance our Italian agent, Antonio Comelli of the Albani Group, will be on the same flight.'

'The Heads of Department will join us for dinner, which has been arranged for 2100 on the 20th.'
'We have laid on dinner at 2100 for nine of us on the 20th.'

'We have reserved a room for you at the Grand.'
'We have booked you into the Grand.'

Notice that you book someone *on* a flight
*into* a hotel
*through* to New York (e.g. from Athens via Rome to New York)

Note how the formal letter in **A1** contains a higher proportion of words which are Latin in origin, such as

'delighted'  'coincidence'  'commitments'  'endeavour'

Note how the second letter in **A1** has a higher proportion of Anglo-Saxon words or phrasal verbs which makes the tone less formal, such as

'pick up'  'laid on'  'tie up'  'try'  'chance'

## B1 Opening and closing phrases for different kinds of letters

The opening and closing phrases are important as they establish the tone of your letter. The following examples would appear in a formal, impersonal letter.

Dear Madam,    Note that the writer does not know the addressee's name nor has he taken the trouble to find it.

Unless we hear from ......    'Unless' is sometimes followed by a threat.

Yours faithfully,    'Yours faithfully' is only written when the salutation is 'Dear Sir' or 'Dear Madam'. It is formal and distant.

## B2 Establishing the tone of a letter

Look at the beginnings and endings of the following four letters and fill in the answers below. When you have decided the main purpose of the letter place a tick ( √ ) in the appropriate column.

Purpose of the letter:

| to | 1 | 2 | 3 | 4 |
|---|---|---|---|---|
| inform | √ | | | |
| apologise | | √ | | |
| threaten | | | √ | |
| sympathise | | | | √ |

1     Dear Mr Craig,
      I am writing to advise you that your account is now ................ so that the situation can be rectified
      Yours sincerely,

Note the formal language which creates distance even though the recipient's name is used.

2     Dear Mrs Ghosh,
      We were very sorry to receive your letter about ..........
      In the meantime, please accept our sincere apologies for the inconvenience we may have caused.
      Yours sincerely.

Note how this letter is formal but an effort has been made to sound friendly.
(very sorry – please accept – we may have caused)

3    Dear Mr Alexis,
     Are you aware that your car has been parked in front of ..........
     I shall have to take the matter further
     Yours truly,

Starting with a question makes this very blunt. The writer ends with a
threat. By signing 'Yours truly', even though he knows Mr Alexis, makes
the letter very cold and formal.


4    Dear Mrs Klein,
     I've only just heard the sad news ..........
     Please let me know if there is anything I can do to help. I'll
     phone you next week.
     With our best wishes,

By the use of contraction (I've – I'll) and the ending, this letter is informal and friendly.


## B3    Exercises in beginning and ending your letter

The opening and closing sentences of the following examples have been
separated. Match up the extracts which belong together.

(a) Dear
    On Friday we're having a few friends round
    to our place for drinks ..........

(b) Dear Sue,
    Thank you for your letter of the 5th. I
    really do think you should have told me
    ..........

(c) Dear Sirs,
    You will surely agree that we have been
    very patient about ..........

(d) Dear Ms Vango,
    Congratulations – we heard today that you
    ..........

(e) Dear Mrs Petersen,
    It was kind of you to ..........

(i)   I will do all I can but you must know you
      have left it very late.
      Yours sincerely,
      Andy Park

(ii)  Our very best wishes for the future.
      Very sincerely yours,
      Margaret Melville

(iii) .......... about 8.30. I hope you can make it.
      Yours,
      Olga

(iv)  Thank you once again.
      Yours sincerely,
      Paul

(v)   If we do not have all the details of the On
      Board Bill of Lading by 28th October we
      shall have to cancel the order.
      Yours faithfully,
      A J Agnew


When you have matched the examples, decide what the purpose of each
letter is.

4

## C1 A memo

Inter-office memos differ from ordinary letters. They are written to people within one company. They follow the basic principles of letter-writing. They are usually more direct, concise and less formal than letters. The opening and closing phrases are omitted. The following memo was sent to the various Heads of Department by Mr Ioannou after he had written to Mr Comelli.

```
To:   JJ   Sales
      AKM  Accounts
    . IL   Advertising        Date:  Sept. 1st
      PJB  Legal              From:  C. Ioannou (MD)
      JD   R & D
      NC   Production
```

Subject : Proposed visit of Mr. Comelli - 19th October

Mr. Comelli is the Import Manager for the entire Albani Group.
He will spend all day in the plant on 20th October.  His
programme is as follows:

| Time | Subject | Participants |
|------|---------|--------------|
| 0930 | Look through last year's results | AKM JJ CI |
| 1000 | Weigh up new products | JJ NC IL CI |
| 1030 | Work out price levels for new products | AKM JJ CI |
| 1100 | Coffee  - | |
| 1115 | Tie up promotional activities | IL NC JJ |
| 1215 | Fix up renewal of agency contract | PJB JJ |
|      | Lunch | |
| 1430 | Visit Quality Control lab to sort out Spring Hotel's complaint in Quality Control lab. | AKM JD JJ CI |
| 1530 | Talk over long-term Research & Development | JJ JD CI |
| 1600 | Look over new high-speed packaging unit | |

All meetings will take place in my office unless specified
to the contrary.  Will participants please brief me in
writing before October 14th?

I hope you will all be able to join us for dinner at the
Grand.  A table has been booked for 2000 hours.

Note how positive Mr Ioannou is in his memo. The language used is direct, concise and less formal than in his letter to Comelli in A1.

## C2   Phrasal verbs

Compare the schedule given in the memo in **C1** with the one given to Mr Comelli in **A1**. What are the one word equivalents of the following phrasal verbs? You will find them all in the original timetable in **A1**.

To look through
> weigh up
> work out
> tie up
> fix up
> sort out
> talk over
> look over

## C3   File memos

Records of telephone calls, visits, conversations, should be kept in File memos. The Director of the Research & Development Department wrote the following memo when he returned from his holiday.

 Fill in the gaps, choosing from the prepositions in the margin on the left. Some prepositions may have to be used more than once.

7 over
6 with
2 in
4 at
on
9 for
3 by
10 of

```
Date:        28th August
From:        LK (R & D)
File:        C 27
Subject:     Albani - Milan


Whilst ..(1).. holiday ..(2).. Zurich last month, I met
Mr & Mrs Abate ..(3).. chance. They were also guests
..(4).. the Royal. Mr. A. is Catering Manager ..(5)..
Springs Hotel (some time ago merged ..(6).. Albani).
Not knowing who I was, the possibility ..(7)..
Albani now being taken ..(8).. was mentioned. No
names were quoted but indicated he knew who it was.

Action:    Check:  1.  Are Albani looking ..(9).. an
                       opening ..(10).. this market?
                   2.  What inside information does
                       AKM have?
```

Note another way of expressing:

 As he did not know who I was, he mentioned ......
 ★ Not knowing who I was, he mentioned ......

 As I did not understand what to do I asked ......
 ★ Not understanding what to do I asked ......

## D1 Telex

Telex is one of the most efficient forms of business communication. It provides a written record, it is immediate, economical and can be sent even when the receiving office is shut. Rates are calculated according to the time taken to transmit the message.

### HINTS

★ When you wish to write a telex, make a draft of what you wish to say and underline the important words which carry the main points.

★ Group questions together.

★ Start a new line or new paragraph when you change the subject.

★ Do *not* abbreviate if you doubt the recipients' knowledge of English.

Here is Mr Comelli's telex in reply to Mr Ioannou's letter of invitation in **A1**.

```
ATTN C IOANNOU
THIS IS TO CFM DET IN YR LTR 18TH AUG.
TKS FOR YR OFFER OF HOSPITALITY.
WE ACCEPT WITH PLEASURE.
RE. SCHEDULE - O.K. I SUGGEST WE ALSO
DISCUSS IMPENDING CHANGES TO LOCAL
FOOD & DRUG LAW. I LOOK FWD TO MEETING
YOU ON 19TH.
REGARDS COMELLI
```

Notice these telex abbreviations.

| | |
|---|---|
| ATTN | for the attention of |
| CFM | confirm |
| DET | details |
| YR | your |
| LTR | letter |
| TKS | thanks |
| FWD | forward |
| RYT or RE YR TLX | referring to your telex |

## D2 Making a discreet enquiry

Only Mr Comelli was expected. In his telex he refers to 'we'. Who is coming with him? His wife, his boss, a colleague?

Read the following telexes carefully. Which is the most polite and tactful – **A, B** or **C**?

**A**

```
RE YR TLX 27TH. ADVISE US DETAILS OF
YR HOTEL REQUIREMENTS.
BRING ALL AVAILABLE INFO. RE FOOD/
DRUG LAW.
REGARDS.
```

**B**

```
RE YR TLX 27TH. REGRET WE DO NOT
UNDERSTAND YOU.
WHO IS COMING WITH YOU?
WE MUST SEE NEW REGULATIONS RE
FOOD & DRUG LAW.
```

**C**

```
TKS FOR YR TLX 27TH.
PLEASE BRING ALL INFO. RE FOOD/DRUG
LAW.
MAY WE ASSUME YOUR WIFE WILL JOIN US
FOR DINNER? PLEASE CONFIRM. REGARDS
```

Note that in **A** the use of the imperatives 'Advise' and 'Bring' is demanding. In **B** the direct question and the use of 'must' are very forceful, but in **C** efforts have been made to be polite and tactful. 'May we assume' is a polite way of saying 'we assume'.

## D3   A telex

Mr Ioannou telexes a business acquaintance in Milan to ask about the rumour mentioned in **C3**.
Note how the following sentence has been abbreviated:

The Director has recently heard rumours about one of their large customers, Albani, being taken over.

```
CONFIDENTIAL

HAVE HEARD RUMOUR ABOUT ALBANI

BEING TAKEN OVER
```

Now abbreviate the following.

Mr Ioannou would like his friend in Milan to investigate the company's background. It must be done with discretion and Mr Ioannou also assures his friend he would treat any report in confidence.

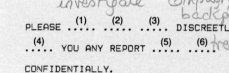

```
                investigate  company's
                                  backgro.
PLEASE .....  .....  ..... DISCREETLY
        (1)   (2)    (3)
 (4)                        (5)    (6)
.....  YOU ANY REPORT .....  ..... treat

CONFIDENTIALLY.
```

## D4   Here is the reply Mr Ioannou received from Milan

```
CONFIDENTIAL

WITH REF YR TLX 18.8 ALBANI UNLIKELY TO BE TAKEN OVER.

FAMILY WISH REMAIN CONTROL. THEY DO NOT APPEAR SHORT

OF CAPITAL. NO REASON WHY YOU CANNOT CONTINUE TRADING.

WILL CONTACT IF FURTHER NEWS.

REGARDS.
```

Change this telex to a letter. Include the following phrases of reassurance:

As far as I can see ...... (taken over).
At present there is no need for concern ......
(family maintain control).
I can assure you ...... (not short of capital).
If I hear anything to the contrary I will contact you.

# UNIT 2

In this Unit you will find:

**A.** A letter of enquiry
**B.** Practice in describing company location
**C.** A letter acknowledging an enquiry
**D.** A letter of refusal

---

## A1 Letter asking for information

Here is a letter written by a company in Bangladesh to a German Trade Attache in Dacca. As you read, consider the comments in the margin.

> Reference JP/AM
>
> 7th April
>
> Dear Sir,
>
> We are an industrial organisation established in 1975 by Government decree and we operate here in Bangladesh.
>
> We are most interested in developing secondary industry in this area. One of our projects is to establish a leather board industry and we wonder if you could help us to find a suitable partner.
>
> The sort of company we have in mind is a large-scale manufacturer of leather board, with international marketing experience and a strong technical staff.
>
> We would be most grateful if you could recommend a German company which fits this description.
>
> Yours faithfully,
>
> *J. Pirani*
>
> J. Pirani
> Director

*In what way could they help?*

*Who would be a suitable partner?*

Notice how Mr Pirani explains what is required:

> We are most interested in/increasing/developing/extending ..........
> We wonder if you could help us/advise us/send us/let us have ..........
> (What) we have in mind is ..........

Other useful phrases include

> What we require is ..........
> What we need is ..........
> We would like you to ..........

Note this common way of ending a letter asking for confirmation.

| We would be most grateful if you could | help advise | us. |
|---|---|---|
| | send give | us ...... |

## A2   Letter of Enquiry

As a result of the Trade Attache's recommendation Mr Pirani wrote to a company in the Federal Republic of Germany. Think about the questions in the margin as you read the letter.

Why did Pirani choose Bruggman GmbH

```
Franz Bruggman GmbH        Ref: JP/AM
Stuttgart
Federal Republic           Date: May 1st
of Germany


Dear Sirs,

Your name has been given to us by the German
Trade Attache in Dacca as one of the most
important leather board manufacturers in
Europe. We are an industrial organisation
```

Who is 'us'?

operating in Bangladesh and would be most
grateful if you could help us.

We have recently been allocated land and
2,000,000 US dollars worth of foreign exchange
in order to improve the country's balance of
payments. One of our projects is to establish
a leather board industry in this area.

What area?

You will appreciate that our technical
knowledge is limited, and we need the
expertise of someone who has experience in
this industry. Would you consider helping us
in any or all of the following ways?

1. Supplying modern machinery.
2. Supplying technical know-how.
3. Helping with the marketing operation.
4. Training personnel.
5. Setting up the plant.

We would like your views on the possibility
of setting up a partnership.

Note that 'know how' means 'practical knowledge'.

Note the various stages of the letter.

### Introduction

'Your name has been given to us as one of the most important leather board manufacturers in Europe.'

Other useful phrases for introducing yourself include:

Your company has been recommended to us by ......
We have heard of your firm ......
We are particularly interested in ......

## Making the request

'You will appreciate that ...... We need ......
Would you consider supplying us with ......?'

Other useful phrases for making a request include:

If you could send/give ......, we would be most grateful.
Could you please let me/us have ......
You will appreciate that we require/need ......

We would like your comments/thoughts on the possibility of | opening ......
becoming ......
entering ......
sharing ......

## Offering further information

We will be only too happy to | supply you with
let you have | more details.

Please do not hesitate to contact us if you require/need further information.

## Ending the letter

We look forward to | hearing from you
meeting you
seeing you

## A3  Practise making an enquiry and booking accommodation

Read this letter.

> Dear Sir,
>
> I would like to reserve a single room with bath
> for the nights of August 14th and 15th.
> I would very much appreciate a quiet room away
> from traffic noise.
> Could you please confirm that there is a lift
> to whichever floor I am on, as I have difficulty
> with stairs?
>
> Yours faithfully,

Now write a similar letter including the following information:

– you require a conference room
– the dates are from August 18th to the 26th
– you need a large room as there are 30 people attending the conference
– you will need to have electric sockets for an overhead projector and a
  screen
– you would like to have confirmation that there will be buffet facilities


## B1   Active and Passive Voice

Misunderstanding, confusion and irritation can be caused by careless use of
the passive voice.

'The goods will be insured from warehouse to warehouse'

If you receive a letter containing this sentence, who, do you think will insure
the goods? It is possible the goods will not be insured by anyone, each
assuming the other will do it. Re-write the sentence above to make the
meaning clear – *You* are the buyer. The seller will insure the goods.

Then complete the blank spaces in the table below. Change the verbs from
the active to the passive voice or vice versa. Make any other alterations
where necessary.

| Active | Passive |
|---|---|
| 1.  You have not *paid your bill* | i.  Your bill has not been paid. |
| 2.  I will *pick him up at 7,00* | ii.  He will be picked up at 0700 hrs. |
| 3.  The board did not *show an immediate interest* | iii.  No immediate interest was shown by the board. |
| 4.  We cannot find any record of this account. | iv.  No record *of this account can be found* |
| 5.  We will have to *cut salary and shorten holidays* *make salary cut* | v.  Salary cuts will have to be made and holidays shortened. |
| 6.  We have made a mistake and incurred a loss. | vi.  A mistake *has been made and ,,* |
| 7.  You have ......... We have made ........ to forward a statement | vii.  Your account has been overdrawn to the extent of £187. Arrangements have been made to have a statement forwarded to you so that your exact position can be checked. |

Note how the sentences in the passive voice can sound more tactful than
when they are written in the active voice.

## B2 Vocabulary – dictionary work

| | consideration | know-how | partner | skills | terms | facilities | prices | manufacturer | |
|---|---|---|---|---|---|---|---|---|---|
| suitable | | | | | | | | | |
| excellent | | | | | | | | | |
| favourable | | | | | | | | | |
| important | | | | | | | | | |
| competitive | | | | | | | | | |
| industrial | | | | | | | | | |
| careful | | | | | | | | | |
| technical | | | | | | | | | |

Look at the grid above. Use your dictionary to check that you know the exact meaning of the adjectives in the column on the left. Decide whether the adjectives in the left hand column can be used with each of the nouns along the top of the grid. If the two words can be used together, put a tick ( √ ) in the relevant box. The phrases that you make are common in business letters.

## B3  Describing a location

Study the following paragraph:

```
Our new Pakistani mill is in Hyderabad.  It is situated in an area
which is scheduled for light industry, one hundred kilometres north-east
of Karachi and one hundred and fifty kilometres south of Khairpur.
```

Check in your dictionary for the correct adjectives for the countries in
column 2 of the table below. For example, Ireland/Irish, Pakistan/Pakistani.

Use the table to write similar paragraphs about each organisation in column 1.

Choose from the following list to complete column 4:
preservation – light industry – heavy industry – conservation –
tourism – leisure and recreation – general industrial use – cultural activities.

| 1 | 2 | 3 | 4 | N | S | E | W |
|---|---|---|---|---|---|---|---|
| Organisation | Country | Town | Scheduled for | | | | |
| Cotton Mill | Ireland | Wexford | Light Industry | | Dublin 112 km | Waterford 32 km | |
| Safari park | Kenya | Kitale | ? | Nairobi 320 km | | Kisumu 120 km | |
| Hotel | Norway | Alesund | ? | | Trondheim 200 km | | Oslo 320 km |
| Sports complex | Scotland | Aviemore | ? | Glasgow 175 km | Inverness 48 km | | |
| Steel Factory | Japan | Nagoya | ? | | | Osaka 180 km | Tokyo 200 km |
| Art Gallery | Spain | Cordoba | ? | Malaga 200 km | | Seville 150 km | |
| Warehouse | Turkey | Izmir | ? | | Istanbul 500 km | | Ankara 750 km |
| Nature Park | Canada | Dog Creek | ? | Vancouver 400 km | | Saskatchewan 150 km | |

## C1  Acknowledging an enquiry

Mr Bremser is the Managing Director of Franz Bruggman in Stuttgart. Read this extract from his letter to Mr Pirani and consider the comments in the margin:

What must Mr Pirani do first?

What would they like to know about the Market?

When would a 'turn-key' contract enable you to start production?

```
Dear Mr Pirani,

Thank you for your letter of 1st May.
We could possibly help you in
establishing a plant in Dacca, but we
regret that we could not enter into any
form of partnership.  However, we are
interested in your project and prior to
working out an offer in detail we need
answers to the following questions :

1.  What volume do you expect over the
    next five years and what quality?
2.  How is the market supplied at present,
    at what price and quality level?
3.  What industrial skills exist?  Is
    there an adequate labour force
    available?
4.  What facilities exist for training
    the labour force?
5.  What safeguards would your
    Government be prepared to enforce
    in order to protect the market?
6.  What is the transport system in the
    area?
7.  What is the present capacity of the
    power supply?
    Have you control over your water supply?

In principle we are interested in supplying
machinery, the necessary technology and
'know-how':  we could in fact offer you a
'turn-key' contract if you wish.
```

Note that 'plant' means 'factory', 'prior to' means 'before' and 'turn-key contract' means a contract for equipment for the complete factory.

Notice how Mr Bremser showed his interest:

> 'We could possibly help you in establishing a plant in Dacca, *but* ......

Then he states the negative point:

> 'But we regret that we could not enter into any form of partnership. However ......'

and he continues with a positive alternative statement:

> 'However, we are interested in your project ......'

The use of connectors such as 'but' and 'however' and 'and' link ideas together and make a letter easier to read. Other useful connectors include:

> nevertheless, as a result, moreover, consequently
> as well as, in spite of (or despite), in fact

These will be practised in **C2**.


## C2  Supplying information

Here are notes Mr Pirani made in order to answer points 1–7 in the letter in **C1**:

```
Output   1st year   -   1500 tons
         2nd  "     -   2000 tons          MOREOVER
rising to around  2500 tons
within 5 years
```

```
Expect 90% - 100%
of production will
be for export
```

Note how these two ideas are linked in the following sentences.

1. In the first year, the output will be 1500 tons, 2000 in the second year, rising to 2500 tons within 5 years. Moreover, we expect that between 90% and 100% of the production will be for the export market.

Now write similar sentences from the following:

```
2. Market supplied only by                        demand for high
   low quality imports at      AS A RESULT         quality
   local current prices
```

At present the market is ................................................................................................

3. DESPITE          unskilled labour force          required number
                                                     skilled operators
                                                     trained after 1 year


**Despite the fact that** .......................................................................................................................


4. Facilities limited          NEVERTHELESS          plans made to
                                                     improve the situation


**At present** .......................................................................................................................


5. Generous tax incentives          IN FACT          40% tariff on all
   for new industries                                imports


**There are** .......................................................................................................................


6. Excellent road and          AS WELL AS          river transport to
   rail services                                   major ports


**We now have** .......................................................................................................................


7. Power station opened          CONSEQUENTLY          have more power than
   last year                                          required - also
                                                       adequate water supply


**A power station** .......................................................................................................................

## D1 Letter of refusal

After the Franz Bruggman Board of Directors had considered Mr Pirani's letter Mr Bremser wrote to Mr Pirani. As you read the letter, think about the comments in the margin.

Dear Mr Pirani,

### Proposed Leather-Board Industry - Dacca

**Acknowledging letter**

**Expressing regret**

Thank you for your detailed letter of June 6th. After careful consideration we regret that we are unable to help you in setting up a special plant for local manufacture.

**Encouraging but giving a reason for refusal**

In theory, your project is an exciting one but we fear that in practice the volume you mentioned is insufficient to justify the necessary investment.

**Offering an alternative: a counter-proposal**

However, if you would like to reconsider the project, you might prefer to act as a distributor of our products in Bangladesh. We would be happy to supply you from our plant in Germany at competitive prices and on favourable terms.

**Ending on a warm note – perhaps they will co-operate in the future**

Thank you again for your enquiry. Should you decide to proceed with your original plan, we would like to wish you every success in the future.

Yours sincerely,

*J. A. Bremser*

J.A. Bremser
(Managing Director)

## D2   Letters of refusal

Reply to the situations below – choose phrases from the appropriate paragraphs in **D1**.

Observe these 4 stages in each letter:

1. Acknowledge.
2. Express regret (be tactful).
3. Give a reason for your refusal.
4. Offer a counter-proposal.

### Situation 1

> You are a manufacturer. Reply to a wholesaler who is unknown to you. He wrote asking for an agency.

Your reply:
- You are unable to offer an agency.
- You already have a representative.
- Offer a sub-agency.
- Offer to supply through your main agent.

### Situation 2

> You are a bank manager. Reply to a newly established importer who wanted a bank loan.

Your reply:
- You are unable to grant a bank loan.
- He had insufficient collateral.
- Counter-proposal. A third party guarantee.
- Offer to grant the loan on favourable terms.

### Situation 3

> You are a financial manager. Reply to an old customer who asked for longer credit for goods he has already received.

Your reply:
- You are unable to grant further credit.
- You have already given him an extension of 60 days beyond normal. Also further orders are due for delivery soon.
- Counter-proposal: payment by Bill of Exchange accepted 120 days from invoice.
- The customer must pay the interest.

# UNIT 3

In this Unit you will find:

**A.** Confirmation of an order and telex requesting action on the order
**B.** A letter of apology and a telex advising delivery
**C.** An insurance claim

---

## A1 Confirmation of an order

Hotel Interiors design and manufacture high-quality furniture. They specialise in refurnishing and re-decorating hotels. Recently, they secured a large contract to refurnish a 40-bedroom extension for an hotel in Jersey.

i. Here is a letter to an Italian supplier, Lanificio Bonardi SRL in Milan, confirming an order for cloth and other furnishings. Fill in the gaps, using the phrases at the end of the letter.

---

```
                Re   :   Order Ref. No. 184/32 May 29th.

   . Dear Signora Caramellino,

    (1)
    ...... the order we discussed on the telephone this morning for the following  :

        Quality    Pieces    Width x Length    Colour    Price

         3707        15       120  x  40         180      6.000

                     22        "        "        172      6.100

                      3        "        "        171      1.300    (CIF London)

    (2)
    ....... it is essential that there should be no colour variation as the material
                                                                  (3)
    must match the carpets which are already in production. ....... that you can
                                       (4)
    deliver to our factory by July 31st ....... Please ship the goods to our clearing

    agent in London, sending him the negotiable documents by air.  No trans-shipment
              (5)                                                        (6)
    please. ....... the fact that the last shipment was badly creased. ....... that the
                                                 (7)
    goods are rolled full width in order .......?  Would you also please confirm the
                                                          (8)
    special terms we agreed by telephone, namely 120 days from .......?

    Yours sincerely,

    J. Wingate

    J. Wingate
    General Manager
```

*this is to confirm* (1)

21

**Phrases**

Could you please check ......
We would like your assurance ......
We must point out ......
the date of invoice.

This is to confirm ......
at the latest.
May we remind you of ......
to avoid a recurrence.


ii.     Specifying details

a.     Note how the writer gave the customer two instructions about shipping the goods.
       1. Ship the goods to the clearing agent.
       2. Send the negotiable documents by air.

       'Please ship the goods to our clearing agent in London, sending him the negotiable documents by air.'

b.     Re-state the following in the same way.

       1. Ask your customer to specify the despatch date, and also to give details of the method of shipment.
       ★ Please ..................... .

       2. Ask the Production Manager to indicate the completion date. He must bear in mind the factory holiday.
       ★ Please ..................... .

       3. Ask your supplier to quote his most favourable terms, and also ask him not to forget your loyalty discount.
       ★ Please ..................... .


iii.    Note how the following has been re-worded.

       The suppliers are reminded that the colour must not vary.
       ★ It is essential that there should be no colour variation.

       If you cannot guess, use your dictionary to find the nouns from the verbs in italics in the following sentences: e.g. corrode – corrosion.

a.     They insisted that the pipes should not *corrode*.
       ★ 'It is essential ..................... .

b.     He demanded that the quality of the drug should not *deteriorate*.
       ★ 'It is vital ..................... in the quality of the drug.'

Notice also

       'The shirts must be guaranteed not to *shrink*.'

c.     It is important that the goods are well packed, and that nothing is broken or stolen.
       ★ 'It is important ...... against b......, and th....... .'

## A2 Confirmation of Order

Complete this confirmation of order form. You will find all the information you require in the letter in **A1**.

---

*Lanificio Bonardi* SRL                                                        MILANO

## CONFIRMATION OF ORDER

| Customer | Order dated | Customer's Reference |
|---|---|---|
| | **Confirmation dated** 4th June | **Our Reference** 8/MI/438 |

| Terms of Payment | Despatch Method |
|---|---|
| | To arrive............................................................... |

| Quality | Colour | Width cm | Piece length | No. of Pieces | Price |
|---|---|---|---|---|---|
| | | | | | |

Special Instructions

Total value...............................................

Signed.......................................................

## A3 Telex requesting action

As the material had not arrived by the end of July, the manager of Hotel Interiors telephoned his shipper. He discovered that the material was already in London, but the shipper needed the documents in order to clear the goods. Where were the documents? An urgent telex had to be sent to Lanificio Bonardi. Write the telex and include the following:

a. Explain what you have heard from your shipper.
   SHIPPER INFORMS US ...................

b. Find out where the documents are. Stress the urgency of the situation.
   IMPERATIVE YOU LOCATE ...................

c. If the documents are still in Italy, they must be sent by Express post immediately to shippers, Duncan & Grant Ltd.
   POST DOCUMENTS EXPRESS ...................

d. Warn Lanificio Bonardi that any demurrage or loss which is incurred will be charged to them.
   DEMURRAGE AND
   CONSEQUENTIAL LOSS ...................

Here is the telex in reply:

```
DOCS NOW AIRMAILED DUNCAN
& GRANT. OUR SINCERE
APOLOGIES. DOCS DELAYED
BY CHAMBER OF COMMERCE FOR
CERTIFICATION.
REGARDS CARAMELLINO
```

## B1 Letter of excuse or apology

i. In any letter of excuse or apology the objective should be to maintain or restore goodwill at minimum cost. A well-handled complaint can be turned to advantage and increase confidence.

Apologise without delay

We are sorry to tell you that ...................
We very much regret that ...................
We must apologise for ...................
Please accept our sincere apologies (formal).

Give some explanation

At present the situation is ...................
We must explain the reason for ...................
What happened was that ...................
The facts are as follows.

Offer a constructive comment

We shall do everything possible to minimise ...................
Leave the matter in our hands. We will contact you when we
...................  .

Close by repeating your apology and offer reassurance:

Once again, we apologise for ...................
We hope that the inconvenience has not been too serious.
We are doing all we can to ...................

ii. It was necessary to inform the hotel in Jersey that there might be a delay
in their order. A new young and inexperienced secretary drafted the
following letter. Think about the comments in the margin.

```
                    Dear Mr. Camard,


                          Re:   Order 184/32

   apology?         I am writing to inform you that the fabric
                    manufacturers are late with their delivery of your
   explanation?     material and our production is being held up.  We
                    shall not be able to despatch your order until
                    October 1st at the very earliest.

                    We will try to improve on this date, but we cannot
constructive comment promise you anything at this stage.  We hope you
                    will understand this situation.


                    Yours sincerely,
```

iii. When the general manager of Hotel Interiors read this draft, he would
not let it be sent. Note comments in the margin – there was no apology,
explanation or constructive comment. Re-write the letter, making the
tone apologetic. Refer to the phrases in **B1** (i), and include the following
information:

  a. There has been a delay in obtaining the material from Italy.
  b. You have arranged to start production in the next few days.
  c. You promise the hotel the order will be in Jersey early in October.

## B2  Strongly worded telex and memo; request for immediate action; polite refusal

i. In spite of the polite letter to the owner of
the Jersey Hotel, this telex was received
in reply:

```
TKS YR LETTER. MOST CONCERNED DELAY.
ESSENTIAL COMPLETE ORDER HERE SEPT
25TH FOR OFFICIAL OPENING OCT 1ST.
INVITATIONS ALREADY ISSUED TO PRESS &
VIPS. IF POSTPONED REGRET MUST HOLD YOU
RESPONSIBLE FOR COSTS.
REGARDS. CAMARD.
```

The style of this telex is very contracted, using
abbreviations such as TKS (thanks) YR (your)
and VIPS (meaning very important persons).

ii. Hotel Interiors were now in a difficult position. The Jersey hotel owed them a large sum of money; if this order was late they might withhold payment. A memo was sent to the Production Manager urging him to speed up the order.

In the following memo there are gaps which must be filled from the alternatives in the margin on the left. Choose the word which carries the most force. Be specific; you wish to convey the sense of urgency.

threatening/proposing
the end of the
month/25th Sept
possibly/probably
may well/might
been cleared/now arrived
should/must
this week/soon
ought to/must

**INTERNAL MEMO**

**From:** General Manager     **Date:** August 3rd

**To:** Production Manager     **Re:** Jersey Contract

URGENT: ORDER NO. 184/34

1. The above client is ..... legal action if this order does not reach him before ..... He would ..... win his case. He already owes us £17,000 which ..... become a bad debt.

2. Cloth from Bonardi has ..... We ..... start production .....

3. Completion date ..... be brought to mid-September, which means working overtime.
Please advise me of the effect of this on all other orders.

*J.W.*

Could you please check stock lines which we could offer as replacement?

'stock lines' are other lines of cloth which they hold in stock in the warehouse.

iii. Here is the reply from the Production Manager:

**MEMO**

From: Production Manager      Date: 4th August

To:     J. Wingate, General Manager   Re: JERSEY CONTRACT

Much as I sympathise with the problem with the Jersey hotel
I must point out that we would not even cover overheads if
we worked continuous overtime on this order.
I have checked and there is nothing suitable in our stock
lines which we could offer as a replacement. Bearing in
mind the holiday period, the earliest date I can give you is
4/5 October. I'm sorry but that is the best I can do.

'cover overheads': they would not receive enough to pay for staff costs, heating etc.

Note how politely the Production Manager refuses the request.
    'Much as I sympathise ..................'
He continues diplomatically
    'I must point out that ..................'
    'I'm sorry but that is the best I can do.'

In view of the urgency of the situation, the Managing Director was consulted on this issue. It was decided that overtime should be worked after all.

## B3   Telex advising delivery

By September 18th the order was finally completed and ready for shipment.

Send a telex to the hotel in Jersey. Make your telex brief but clear. Include points 1.–4.

1. Ten large packing cases will be despatched from the factory on September 20th. The order has been completed in full.
Reduce this information to *six words*.
e.g. DESPATCHING COMPLETE ORDER SEPTEMBER 20TH.

Now do the same with the following:
2. The cases will be sent by ship on the SS Mariana. The boat is due to sail on September 22nd from Southampton.
(SENDING .................. SAILING ..................)
3. All the documents and invoices will be sent by airmail to the hotel. They will be sent on the day of sailing.
(AIRMAILING ..................)
4. Hotel Interiors will insure the shipment. The goods will be covered for the CIF value plus 10%.
(INSURING .................. PLUS 10%)

## C1  An Insurance Claim

i. Earlier in the year, Hotel Interiors had sent a consignment of furniture including 20 chairs to the North of England. Unfortunately, not all the chairs arrived, and the transport company was held responsible.

Here is the claim form the transport company submitted to its insurance agent. Read it carefully, then answer the questions at the end of the form.

### GOODS IN TRANSIT

Policy No.    843 021

Name of insured ...Thompsons Trucks...
Address............18 The Mint Yard...
...............St Stephen's Gate...
...............Westhampton...
Tel. No. ...24246...
Consignors....Hotel Interiors PLC...
Address.........108 Hickstead Road...
...............Westhampton...
Consignees......Brampton Hospital...
Address.........Scotby Road...
...............Brampton...

If theft or loss, which Police Station was advised and when?

...............................................

If damaged, where are the damaged goods now? ...............................

...............................................

Are there other policies covering the consignment in question?
~~YES~~/NO

Gross amount of claim £...560...
Salvage value if any £................................
Net amount of claim £................................

Number of vehicle ......HJ 660Y...
Make of vehicle ......Leyland...
Date of occurrence...Jan 14/15...
Name of Driver......Peter Ross...
Age ......25...
Length of service ...2 Years...
Name of witness......
Address......

...............................................

Date on which goods collected
          14th January
...............................................
Date on which goods delivered
          15th January
...............................................
Signature given on collection?
   YES/~~NO~~ ✓
Name of signatory ......Peter Ross...
Was receipt clear/~~claused~~?
Signature obtained on delivery
   YES/~~NO~~ ✓
Name of signatory ......M Banks...
~~Clear~~/claused ......4 chairs short...
Nature of load......Furniture...
No. of items in load ......30...
Weight......
Nature of goods lost/damaged
          4 chairs
...............................................
Amount of loss/damage £...560...

I/We declare the foregoing particulars to be true in every respect.

Signature ......Joe Clark.......

Date ......20th January...

Position ......Transport Manager...

Please complete the statement of claim overleaf. Please turn over.

*Note:* The receipt was signed, and a comment was added about the missing chairs. Therefore the receipt was 'claused'.

ii.  Answer the following questions:

    a.  Who sent the chairs?
    b.  Who were the chairs sent to?
   •c.  What happened to the chairs?
    d.  How much did the chairs cost?
    e.  What is the total amount being claimed?
    f.  When the driver examined the consignment in Westhampton was everything in order?
    g.  Was the consignment checked when the chairs were delivered?
    h.  What comment was made in the delivery note which caused it to be 'claused'?

## C2  Questions: making enquiries

When the driver discovered the chairs were missing he telephoned the Head Office. Here is a transcript of their conversation.

The driver's answers in column B are in the correct sequence – the transport manager's questions in column A are not.

Re-arrange the questions to match the answers.

For example,  **Manager:** 'Where are you speaking from?' (d)
                     **Driver:** 'Brampton'  (1)

| **Transport Manager** | **Truck Driver** |
|---|---|
| A | B |
| a.  When did you find out? | 1.  Brampton. |
| b.  Were they all there when you dropped your first load in Manchester? | 2.  No it isn't. That's why I'm ringing. |
| c.  What's the matter? | 3.  I'm four chairs short. |
| d.  Where are you speaking from? | 4.  Only a few minutes ago. |
| e.  Where else did you stop? | 5.  Yes, they were, as far as I know. |
| f.  Is everything O.K.? | 6.  I never left the truck. |
| g.  How else could they have vanished? | 7.  I didn't stop anywhere else. I drove straight here from Manchester. |
| h.  Did you leave the truck at all? | 8.  Well, yes, I did stop for a quick bite to eat, but I had my eye on it the whole time. I never saw anything suspicious at all. |
| i.  You must have left it unlocked somewhere at some time. | 9.  I've really no idea. |

## C3    A statement or claim

Here is an extract taken from the Transport Manager's statement. In order
to complete the gaps, you may need to refer to **C2** as well as the list of words
in the left-hand margin.

*3* denied

*2* questioned

*4* insisted

*1* reported

*6* protested

*5* maintained

```
The driver telephoned me on the 15th January.
He .....(1) that when he unloaded in Brampton, he
found four chairs missing.  When .....(2) he
.......(3) that he had ever left the truck.  He
.........(4) that he had not stopped anywhere
en route and .......(5) that he had never seen
anything suspicious.  Even when he stopped for
lunch he ..........(6) that the lorry was not
out of his sight at any time.
```

# UNIT 4

In this Unit you will find:

**A.** Letters offering congratulations
**B.** Letters about bad debts
**C.** Letters pressing for payment and asking for extended credit

---

## A1  Offering Congratulations

Hotel Interiors plc is a large manufacturing company. It specialises in high quality furniture and interior design for hotels. The chief designer, Paula Durand, has recently been invited to join the Board of Directors.

This formal letter of congratulation to Paula is from the ex-chairman of Hotel Interiors.

Note the formality of the ex-chairman's letter. Compare the formal phrases with the informal equivalents.

'Your appointment gave me great pleasure.'
★ I was very glad to hear about ...................
(*less formal*)

'I offer you my sincere congratulations.'
★ Congratulations! (*less formal*)

'I am delighted that your talent and hard work have been rewarded.'
★ I know how hard you have worked, and you certainly deserve it.

'I had hoped that I might be able to congratulate you in person.'
★ It is a great pity that we can't get together soon.

'When I return in September I will contact you.'
★ I'll give you a ring when I get back.

'In the meantime, I wish you every success.'
★ Meanwhile, all the very best for the future.

Dear Ms Durand,

Your appointment to the Board gave me great pleasure, <u>and I offer you my sincere congratulations</u>. <u>I am delighted</u> that your talent and hard work have been rewarded.

I had hoped that <u>I might be able to congratulate you in person</u>, but I am shortly going on holiday. When I return in September I will contact you and I hope we shall have the opportunity of celebrating. <u>In the meantime</u>, I wish you every success.

Yours Sincerely,

## A2    An informal letter of congratulation

A friend and colleague of Paula's, Steven
Wilson, was recently appointed General
Manager of his Company. Complete Paula's
letter of congratulation to Steven. Refer to **A1**
in order to fill in the gaps in the following letter.

Make your letter informal and personal.

```
    Dear Steven

    I was very ..... ..... about your
    recent appointment.  I know how
    ..... ....., and you certainly
    ..... .......  It is a ..... .....
    I'm going to the States for two
    weeks but ..... ..... when I
    ..... .......  Meanwhile, .....
    .......


    Yours very sincerely,

         Paula
```

## A3    Exercise

Write a letter or a telex to each of the people
shown in the list below.

a.  Your agent in New York, out of hospital
    after a severe illness.
b.  A customer, on the opening of a large new
    factory.
c.  A young relative who has just won a
    Fulbright Scholarship. (A Fulbright
    Scholarship is a prestigious American
    Scholarship.)
d.  Your ex-boss/professor who has just
    become a Member of Parliament.
e.  A college friend who has just had a first
    baby, a daughter.

Here are some more phrases you may find
useful.

> I understand from my colleagues that you
> ...... (*formal*)
> I recently heard the news that ...... (*less
> formal*)
> I have just heard the splendid news ......
> (*less formal*)
> Great news! I was/am thrilled to hear ......
> (*informal*)

## B1 Credit Control

One of Paula Durand's most successful projects was the contract she secured for the re-furnishing of a small but luxurious hotel in Jersey. In September she read in the trade press that such hotels were losing their share of the market. As a result she sent the following memo to her credit controller. Think about the questions in the margin as you read it.

### INTERNAL MEMO

To:    Financial Director B.M.
          Credit Controller M.J.H.

From:  P Durand

Date:  25th Sept

*What is in a difficult situation?*

The financial press reports that many new hotels and restaurants are on shaky ground and there may be bankruptcies occurring.

*What action should the company take?*

1) We must tighten up on our credit terms and collection activities.

2) We must aim to reduce our average

*Collection of what?*

   collection period from the present 60 days to 40 days - or better.

*What could happen?*

Even with these controls we may get caught!
I am concerned about the hotel in Jersey. They have been given generous credit.
Please report what specific measures you are taking.

Note that the phrase 'on shaky ground' refers to financial not structural stability. You will often find figurative phrases like this in financial reports; for instance 'flexible' means that the price of a certain share on the Stock Exchange has fluctuated during the day's trading. Paula Durand refers to the hotel (a singular noun) as 'they'. This is because she is thinking of the people involved rather than the institution.

## B2  Collection Letters

Here are some extracts taken from standard letters sent out to different customers after 30 to 60 days from the agreed date of payment.

When you have read all the following extracts carefully, decide which you would send to

a. a customer who has been valuable to you in the past, but for some reason has not settled his account.
b. a customer who is a *very* slow payer, but who has always paid eventually.
c. a customer whom you feel is a bad risk.

**Extract 1**

> You have not replied to our letters of January 18th
>
> or February 22nd and we have been instructed by
>
> our accounts department to insist on immediate
>
> payment of this overdue account.
>
> An amicable settlement is preferable to us, but
>
> no hesitation will be shown should formal
>
> proceedings become necessary.
>
> Your cheque should be sent to this office at the
>
> above address by return.

Note the tone of 'You have not replied.' This is accusing. In the phrases 'We have been instructed by' and 'to insist on', 'instructed' and 'insist' are *strong* words.

The use of the passive voice makes the unpleasant task of collecting bad debts impersonal and official.
The formal use of 'amicable' maintains distance.

Note the phrase 'no hesitation will be shown'.
This introduces a strong threat.
Note also that the demand 'Your cheque *should* be sent' is not a request but an order.

**Extract 2**

> We do not appear to have received payment for the
>
> invoices listed below:
>
> RD 78659    £56.50
>
> FE 567      £45.75
>
> We should therefore be pleased if you would forward
>
> payment by return of post or alternatively notify us
>
> of any problems you may have concerning these invoices.
>
> The enclosed statement includes a balance brought
>
> forward from December 31st although the agreed credit
>
> facilities require monthly settlement.
>
> It would be appreciated if you could arrange for
>
> settlement to be sent in the course of the next few days.
>
> If payment is already in transit please ignore this letter.

In this extract note the phrases 'We do not appear to have received', 'We should therefore be pleased' and 'It would be appreciated if you could'.

These phrases are tactful and diplomatic. They are also definite without being aggressive. The recipient is well aware of the situation and of what action he must take.

**Extract 3**

> Despite our recent requests for payment your account
>
> is long overdue. Can you ensure that settlement is
>
> made by return of post in order to prevent further
>
> correspondence and inconvenience? If you have already
>
> paid this account, please ignore this letter and accept
>
> our apologies.

Compare this with the previous example in Extract 2. You will note that the Extract 3 above is more direct, less polite. The words 'despite', 'long overdue', 'ensure', 'by return of post' and 'prevent.........inconvenience' are very direct.

## B3  Extracts from collection letters at different stages

The following extracts, written by a collection agent, were sent to customers at various intervals after payment was due.

### Extract 1
When you have read this extract, answer the questions.

```
Your failure to clear this account has forced us

to recommend to our client that they take further

action now.

A cheque sent to my attention within 48 hours can

halt proceedings.

Make your remittance payable to Gunn & Shawcross

and send to the address above.
```

   i.  What are the strong emotive words in this letter?
  ii.  At what stage would you send this letter? After letter 1, 2 or 3 in **B2**?
 iii.  Would you continue to do business with this customer in the future?

### Extract 2
Now compare the extract you have just read with this example.
This is a letter from an accounts department.

```
We have been advised that no payment has been

received for invoice 1098/8 for £156.05.

We are sure this must have escaped your

attention and we must ask you to settle the

account by return.
```

i. How strong does this letter feel to you?
ii. At what stage do you think it was sent?
   After letter 1, 2 or 3 in **B2**?
iii. What was the relationship between the
   writer and the recipient? Was the recipient a
   regular customer, a valued customer or a
   bad security risk?
iv. What could you change in the last sentence
   to:
   a. Make it softer?
   b. Make it sharper?

Use formulae from letters 1, 2 or 3 in **B2**.


## Extract 3
Here is a letter from the legal department of a large store.

> In view of your persistent default your credit
>
> facilities are hereby withdrawn.
>
> We further notify you that if the overdue sum
>
> of £277.00 is not received within ten days
>
> of the date of this letter the local County
>
> Court will issue a summons against you for
>
> the recovery of the above amount plus such
>
> costs as are involved.

i. At what stage was this letter sent? After
   letter 1, 2 or 3 in **B2**?
ii. Re-write this letter making it possible to
   continue business with this customer. Use
   formulae from letter 1, 2 or 3 in **B2**.

## C1 A confidential credit rating report

Hotel Interiors asked a credit rating bureau to supply an up-to-date credit report on the hotel in Jersey. Various suppliers were asked to give their opinion of the hotel's payment habits. The following passage refers to Company A in the confidential report.

Company 'A' has been a supplier for 12 years and has supplied goods on monthly credit to a limit of £20,000. They report that the agreed terms are sometimes exceeded without prior arrangements.

Use the information given in Sections 1, 2, 3 and 4 of the confidential report and write similar paragraphs about the views of companies B, C and D on the hotel.

### CONFIDENTIAL REPORT

Company's History  :  Started five years ago

Registered as a private company.

Present situation:        Payment terms exceeded

Suppliers currently report:-

Section

| | 1 | 2 | 3 | 4 |
|---|---|---|---|---|
| | Length of time known | Comments on payments | Terms agreed | Average credit |
| Company A | 12 years | Terms sometimes exceeded without prior arrangement | Monthly | £ 20,000 |
| Company B | 5 years | Experiencing temporary cash flow problems | 60 days | £ 10,000 |
| Company C | 2 years | Recently terms exceeded – supplies had to be stopped. | 90 days | £ 3,000 |
| Company D | 9 months | Hotel normally pays after second reminder | 30 days | £ 2,000 |

## C2 Pressing for payment

Having received the report, the credit controller decided to send a personal letter to the owner of the hotel.

Choose from the words in the left hand margin to fill the gaps.

breakdown

originally

despite

arrange

specially

touch

understanding

to date

reason

in full

settled

```
                                              28th October

Dear M. Camard,
          Re: Invoices 24/541 July 31st.   £4,000
                       24/555 August 31st. £12,000
                          (1)
I am sorry to see that ..... our previous requests,
                                            (2)
the above accounts have still not been ..... We
wrote to you in August and in September, but have
                        (3)            (4)
received no payment ..... When we ..... negotiated
                          (5)                    (6)
the contracts we gave you ..... low prices on the .....
that payments would be made within 30 days of the date
                      (7)
of invoice. Here is a ..... of the situation as it
stands today:-
                    Invoice
July 31st        839/C     £ 4,500   Overdue
August 31st      921/G     £12,000   Overdue
September        980/G     £ 1,800   Now due
October          0210/C    £ 4,000   Due November 30th
                           £22,300
                      (8)
Could you please ..... for the July and August amounts
                (9)
to be paid ..... and for the cheque to be sent to this
office before Monday November 10th.
              (10)                              (11)
If for any ..... this cannot be done, please get in .....
with me immediately.
Yours sincerely,

M. J. Hahn
```

39

## C3   Asking for an extension of credit

i.  The Manager of the hotel in Jersey needs more time to settle his bill with
Hotel Interiors. Here is the letter he wrote to the credit controller of
Hotel Interiors asking for an extension of credit.

As you read the letter through, try to guess what words or phrases would fill
the gaps. When you have decided, check your answer with the explanation
at the end of the letter.

Remember that you wish to make your letter as tactful and as positive as
possible.

```
Dear Mr. Hahn,

        Ref: Your letter 28.10.  JH/Ch

Thank you for your letter of October 28th.  We ....(1)...
.... your concern, and would like to assure you that we
shall ....(2).... to settle our account with you in the
immediate future.  We wish to ....(3).... the following:

Invoice 839/C,  921/G and 980/G - an immediate part payment
of £7,000, the balance to be paid by cheque post-dated to
December 1st.
Invoice 0210/C - We ....(4).... a six month's extension of
credit, on which we will pay interest.
As you know, there have been problems with our expansion
programme, but these have now been ....(5)......
We are now refusing any more bookings for Christmas as we
are fully booked.  We have recently ....(6)... a substantial
contract for a series of conferences to be held throughout
the coming year.  We have also been given a large booking
from an international tour operator.

In view of all these prospects we ....(7)..... that we shall
be able to clear any outstanding debts.

Thank you for your ....(8)..... and patience, also for the
excellent service your company has given us in the past.

Yours sincerely,

Canard.
```

Any of the following words and phrases are acceptable, but there is a subtle difference between the alternatives given.

1. (a) are aware of
   (b) understand
   (c) fully appreciate

(c) is the most tactful and conveys a greater degree of understanding.

2. (a) try
   (b) endeavour
   (c) make every effort

(a) does not convey much determination. (b) is stronger and more formal. (c) indicates sincerity and willingness, but without a definite commitment.

3. (a) suggest
   (b) propose

(a) is not definite enough in this context. (b) shows much firmer intention.

4. (a) want
   (b) need
   (c) require
   (d) would like

(a) is very demanding and blunt (b) and (c) are not as tactful as (d).

5. (a) sorted out
   (b) settled
   (c) resolved

(a) and (b) are not as formal as (c).

6. (a) negotiated
   (b) secured
   (c) signed

(a) does not indicate if the contract was obtained. (b) and (c) show that the contract is finalised.

7. (a) are confident
   (b) hope
   (c) expect

(a) shows the most positive attitude.

8. (a) help
   (b) understanding
   (c) assistance

(a) and (b) are warm and friendly. (c) is more formal.

ii. Use the Credit Controller's letter as a guide to write four similar letters in the situations below. You are being pressed for payment. Explain why you are having difficulties, and make an alternative suggestion.

| *The reason why you cannot pay:* | *Suggest:* |
| --- | --- |
| 1. Sales not up to forecast – prospects bright | Post dated cheques |
| 2. Imported machinery delayed | Return goods? |
| 3. Fire held up production – incurred losses | Bill of Exchange Third Party Guarantee |
| 4. Debtors are slow to pay you | Payment by instalments within 6 months, plus interest |

# UNIT 5

In this Unit you will find:

**A.** Letters of invitation
**B.** Letters of acceptance
**C.** Letters declining an invitation or altering the arrangements
**D.** A press release

## A1  Letters of invitation

Invitations vary from the very formal, gilt-edged card which must be answered in writing to the informal telephone call which requires no written reply.

Here is a semi-formal letter from Professor Marsh, an ecologist, who has been asked to organise a survey of the rain-forests in Brunei. Professor Marsh met Dr Adelby at a conference where she was a guest speaker. She is a lecturer in Economic Geography in Sweden. Read the letter carefully and note the comments on the structure of the letter in the margin.

|  |  |
|---|---|
|  | Dear Dr Adelby, |
| General courtesies | I hope you had a comfortable journey back after the conference. Thank you once again for amost stimulating lecture; it was much appreciated. Perhaps you remember |
| A polite introduction | the conversation we had about Brunei. As you know, a colleague, Tony Spaventa, and I have been working on possibilities of a six-week geological and ecological survey of the Temburong area. I remember you expressed interest in the project. |
| The object of the letter | At last we have received permission and I have been asked to recruit a team. If this can be done in time, we will leave in September. Would you be interested in joining us? I realise this is perhaps short notice, and you may have other commitments, but I do hope you will be able to accept. I can assure you that it will be most interesting and exciting from all points of view. I ought to add that, |
| Giving more details | although the assignment is not particularly well paid, all out-of-pocket expenses will be met. There will also be a |

42

| | |
|---|---|
| | generous overseas allowance. |
| Asking for a response | Could you let me know as soon as possible if you are interested in principle.  Should you be able to join us, full details and a draft contract will be forwarded in due course. |
| Finalising | If all goes according to plan, we may well spend six weeks in the forest region.  This should enable us to produce a survey, an analysis and to make recommendations. |
| | Do let me know when you plan to come to England again.  I look forward to hearing from you. |
| | Yours sincerely, |

Professor Marsh does not present his invitation in the first sentence. He opens with a few polite introductory remarks.

> 'I hope you had a comfortable journey.'
> 'Thank you once again......'
> '......it was much appreciated.'

He goes on to refresh Dr Adelby's memory.

> 'Perhaps you remember ......'
> 'As you know ......'
> 'I remember you expressed interest in ......'

Then he comes to the purpose of the letter.

> 'I have been asked ......'
> 'If this can be done ......'
> 'Would you be interested in ......'

To be diplomatic, he adds

> 'I realise this is perhaps short notice ......'
> '...... you may have other commitments ......'

This is how he tries to persuade Dr Adelby:

> 'I can assure you ...... it will be ......'

and how he warns her about the pay:

> 'I ought to add ......'

He ends

> 'Could you let me know as soon as possible'
> 'Do let me know when you plan to ......'

Towards the end of the letter there are a number of conditional sentences. To avoid using 'if' too many times, note how he used 'should'

> 'If you are able to join us ......'
> 'Should you be able to join us ......'

Now summarise Professor Marsh's letter in not more than 50 words. The following verbs may help you. They are often used when reporting what someone else has said.

referred (lecture) ...... reminded (conversation) ...... invited (to join) ...... outlined (expedition) ...... warned (not well paid) ...... explained (next step) ...... asked (when next in Britain) ......

## A2   An informal invitation

Professor Marsh also wrote an informal note to his old friend and colleague
Tony Spaventa, in America, inviting him to join the team. Compare this
letter with the formal one to Dr Adelby. Note the idiomatic expressions.
Professor Marsh is writing as he would speak.

> Dear Tony,
>
> Did all go well with your return journey? I hope so. Remember
> our talk about Brunei with Karen Adelby? I've just heard
> that we can go ahead. Can you join us?
>
> I know this doesn't give you much time and you may have
> got fixed up for the Autumn, but I do hope you can
> make it.
>
> The aim is to get away by mid-September. I promise
> you it will be exciting even if there is not much money
> in it. All expenses will be covered, of course.
>
> If you can join us please let me know by return. I'll
> contact you as soon as I get more details.
>
> Yours in haste,
>
> Peter.

Refer back to the letter written to Dr Adelby and note the formal
equivalents for the following idiomatic expressions:

'Did all go well with your return journey?'
'I hope you had a comfortable journey back after the conference.'

'Remember our talk about Brunei with Karen Adelby?'
'Perhaps you remember the conversation we had about Brunei?'

'I have just heard that we can go ahead.'
'At last we have received permission ......'

'...... you may have got fixed up for the autumn ......'
'...... you may have other commitments ......'

'...... I do hope you can make it.'
'...... I do hope you will be able to accept.'

'...... there is not much money in it.'
'...... the assignment is not particularly well paid ......'

Note the use of short sentences and contractions such as 'I'll' in a hand-written letter. Usually these contractions would be changed to the full form by the person typing the letter.

## B1  A semi-formal acceptance

When Dr Adelby received Professor Marsh's letter she telephoned him from Sweden. Later she wrote the following letter. As she had spoken to him on the telephone, she addressed him by his first name.

---

Dear Peter,

This is just to confirm Monday's telephone conversation. I am delighted to accept your invitation to take part in the Brunei project. Thank you very much for thinking of me.

I heard today that I have to be in Oxford on Thursday 16th February. I could meet you in London either on the 15th, Wednesday evening, or on the 17th, Friday morning. Which would be most convenient? It would be an excellent opportunity to get down to some detailed planning. I shall be staying at the Europa Hotel, Charlton Street.

I hope that Tony Spaventa will be able to join us. I was most impressed with his article in "The Scientific Journal." His experience would be invaluable in Brunei.

Let me know about the 15th or 17th. I look forward to meeting you again.

Yours sincerely,

Karen Adelby

---

Notice how Dr Adelby accepts the invitation.
'I am delighted to accept your invitation to take part in the Brunei project.'
Here are two similar phrases.
'I am (very) pleased to accept the invitation.'
'Thank you for your invitation, which I am pleased to accept.'

## B2 A telex accepting an invitation

Tony Spaventa sent the following telex from Barbados.

```
ATTN. MARSH
MANY THANKS YOU LETTER 18TH. GREAT NEWS.
DELIGHTED TO ACCEPT. HAVE APPLIED FOR EIGHT
WEEKS LEAVE FROM SEPT 1ST. LOOK FWD TO FURTHER
DETAILS ASAP. AM VISITING LONDON APRIL 7TH
THROUGH 18TH. CAN WE MEET? LETTER FOLLOWING.
BEST REGARDS TONY
```

Note the use of the American 'through'.
This includes both 7th and 18th April.

## B3 Informal acceptance

Now fill in the gaps in the following letter. Choose the appropriate words from the left-hand margin.

fairly
to confirm
many thanks
as though
sort out
get in
contact
let me

Dear Peter,

This is just ...(1)... my telex ...(2)... for your invitation.
It looks ...(3)... I will be able to join you in Brunei
after all.

I have yet to ...(4)... the question of dates, as I'm not
really due more than 28 days leave, however I am ...(5)...
confident.

I shall be in London on 7th. I'll ...(6)... you at the office
when I ...(7)... about 9.30 a.m. on Monday and you can
...(8)... have more details then. Thanks once again.

Yours in great haste,

*Tony*

Note that for most people

'fairly confident' = 60–70% certain,
'reasonably confident' = 70–80% certain,
'pretty confident' = 80–90% certain,
'absolutely confident' = 100% certain.

46

## C1 Declining an invitation and suggesting alternative arrangements

Peter cannot meet Karen on February 15th or 17th. Read the following letter
in which he makes an alternative suggestion.

```
          Dear  Karen,


          Thank you for your letter of January 20th. I am very

          sorry that I cannot meet you on either 15th or 17th as

          you suggested.  I have to be in Paris that week.  It is

          a long-standing engagement which I am afraid I cannot

          alter.

          Would it be possible to meet on Saturday 18th instead?

          I could collect you from your hotel at 11.30 a.m.  I

          would be very happy to show you round the Research Unit

          after lunch.  We would have time to draw up some sort of

          schedule for the trip.

          If this is not convenient, please don't hesitate to contact

          me on 01-246-8007.

          I look forward to meeting you again.

          Yours sincerely,
```

How you decline an invitation depends on the degree of formality which
exists between the two parties. Here are some phrases that can be used if the
invitation is formal.

| Thank you for your invitation, but | I regret I am unable to meet you. |
| | it is unfortunate that I shall not be able to attend the meeting. |
| | I very much regret that I cannot come. |

If the invitation is semi-formal, these phrases may be used.

| Thank you for your invitation, but | I am very sorry I shall not be able to come. |
| | although I would much like to accept I cannot. |

You may want to offer an excuse:

This is due to a | previous long-standing prior |, engagement.

Circumstances have changed since I last | saw you. heard from you. wrote to you.

The position has now altered.

Unfortunately, I have to ......

Here are some ways of suggesting an alternative:

Would it be | possible to ...... convenient to ......

Can I suggest ......

I would like to suggest ......

and in case the alternative is not acceptable:

If this is not convenient, please telephone me on ......
If this is not convenient, please don't hesitate to contact me.

## C2  Altering arrangements

Use the framework of the letter which follows to write to these people.

a.  to your Bank Manager:

You had an appointment with him next week, on Tuesday at 1600 hrs to discuss your overdraft. Now you want to change the time to 1400 hrs as you have an unexpected Board Meeting.

b.  to a colleague:

You had a lunch appointment for 12.45 next Friday but you have to go to Paris for a meeting on Thursday. Suggest an alternative date, time and place to meet.

Choose the most appropriate phrase. One letter is formal, the other less formal.

Dear ......,

| I sincerely regret<br>I regret that<br>I'm sorry | I shall be unable to keep our | appointment<br>date |

on .......... at ..........

| I | tried<br>attempted | to | get hold of<br>contact | you on the telephone but |

.......... (make your excuse) ..........

| Would it be possible<br>Can we fix up | another time? |

| Would .......... on .......... at .......... be | possible<br>convenient for you? |

| Yours sincerely<br>With best wishes |

Now write either a letter or a telex for the following situations.

| An appointment was arranged | with | Excuse and proposal |
|---|---|---|
| 1. 12.30 next Monday in London. | A French customer who will only be in your city for 2 days | You have a prior appointment. Suggest 2 alternatives. |
| 2. 12.00 next Tuesday in prospective employer's office. | A prospective employer | Make your own excuse. Say you'll leave it to him to suggest another appointment |

## D1    A Press Release

The National Press would like information about the survey. They want to know *facts*.

The Overseas Development Organisation issued the following press release which was sent to the national newspapers. Note the formal, factual style of writing. Think about the questions in the left hand margin as you read the press release.

Does he always work for
the O.D.O.?

What sort of work do
you think she did?

What sort of work does
Tony do?

## PRESS RELEASE

### OVERSEAS DEVELOPMENT ORGANISATION
SURVEY OF TEMBURONG

Permission has now been obtained from the relevant authorities for a geological and ecological survey of the little-known Temburong district of north-west Brunei.

The survey is taking place later this year and will be financed by the Overseas Development Organisation.

The party consists of:

*Professor Peter Marsh* Ph.D. B.Sc. an ecologist who has been seconded to the O.D.O. by the Land and Agricultural Organisation.
*Doctor Karen Adelby* Fil.mag., winner of the TAKAR PRIZE last year for her work in Peru. She is a lecturer in Economic Geography, at present working in Sweden.
*Doctor Tony Spaventa* Ph.D. an American geologist who is at present working with Morrison Mining Enterprises. He specialises in geological mapping and aerial surveying.

The team leaves England on September 22nd and returns from Brunei six weeks later.

It will be appreciated that many details have yet to be finalised. For this reason we are arranging a final press conference on Monday September 18th when all members of the survey will be present and full details will be available to the Press.

Issued by the Press Office

To extract as much information as possible, journalists at a press conference often ask questions which begin with 'Who' 'Where' 'What' 'When' 'Why' 'How' 'How much' and 'How many'. You cannot answer 'Yes' or 'No' to these questions. If they ask questions using 'Do' 'Does' 'Is' 'Are' 'Can' 'Have' 'Will' etc., short 'Yes' or 'No' responses may be given. They may need to ask further questions to get the information they require. Make a list of 15 questions which are answered by this press release. Use the 'Wh' and 'How' questions where possible

e.g. Who granted permission?

Now write a press release either about your own company or about any other organisation to which you belong. Anticipate the questions that journalists are likely to ask, and try to give answers to as many potential questions as possible.

## D2   Choosing the correct preposition

Which prepositions in the horizontal line are most often used with the phrase or sentence in the vertical column on the left? You may find that you can use more than one preposition with each phrase. Fill in the matrix with one or more ticks ( √ ) where necessary.

| | ON | FOR | BY | WITH | OF | AT | TO | ABOUT | IN |
|---|---|---|---|---|---|---|---|---|---|
| 1. The survey is being financed ......... | \ | | X | X | | | | | |
| 2. The team consists ......... | o | | | X | X | | | X | |
| 3. He has been authorised ......... | \ | | X | | | | X | | |
| 4. Peter is a lecturer ......... | | | | | | ✓ | | | |
| 5. Tony specialises ......... | | | | | | | | | X |
| 6. Dr Adelby works ......... | X | X | | X | | X | | | X |
| 7. We had a most interesting discussion ......... | X | | | | | | | X | |
| 8. The Press shows an interest ......... | | X | | | | | X | X | |
| 9. Permission has been granted ......... | | | | | | | | | |
| 10. They met ......... coincidence | | | X | | | | | | |
| 11. We are now looking forward ......... | | | | | | | X | | |

# UNIT 6

In this Unit you will find:

**A.** Note taking and report writing
**B.** Memos and recommendations
**C.** Statistical vocabulary

---

## A1    Note taking

Here are some brief notes made by a store detective, one of whose duties is to protect the store from shoplifters. Read them carefully. As you read, think about the questions in the margin. Note how to save time and space, parts of speech are omitted.

Pronouns?

Articles?

Sequencing phrases?

Connection?

Parts of verbs?

> May 18th — 5pm — 4th Floor
>
> Saw nervous young man, kept him under observation. He approached leather jackets. Tried on brown one, placed it on chair near exit, crossed to raincoats. Tried on several, returned to jacket left on chair. Put it on. Followed him downstairs. He left by the main door. Stopped him outside. First denied, then admitted he had not paid. Police called, incident reported.

In a report or when making an official statement, it is important to indicate the logical sequence of events. This can be done by using connectors such as First – Subsequently – Finally.

In the following extract from the detective's statement to the police, the connectors have been left out. Choose the appropriate ones from the list to fill in the gaps.

| a while | later | later |
|---|---|---|
| To begin with | previously | due course |
| subsequently | after which | finally |
| initially | first | After |

52

I decided to keep him under observation. ......(1)..... he approached

a rail full of leather jackets. After .....(2)..... he tried on a

brown one, ...(3).. he placed it on a chair near the exit. A few

moments ...(4).. he crossed over to another display of coats. He

...(5).. tried on several, .....(6)..... he returned to the jacket which

he had ...(7).. left on the chair. He put the jacket on. In ...(8)..

..... I followed him downstairs. He left by the main entrance.

I challenged him outside the store. In the ...(9).. instance he

denied that he had taken anything, but ...(10).. he admitted that he

had not paid for the jacket he was wearing. ...(11).. persuasion, he

reluctantly agreed to return to the store. The police were called

and ...(12).. Mr Anthony Mitchell was charged with shoplifting.

## A2   A report

A report may only be a brief paragraph or many pages long. It may be formal or informal. Here are some extracts taken from a formal report written by a family counsellor about the parents of the young man who was charged with shoplifting. A counsellor is a person who advises someone who is in trouble. For example, at some schools and universities teachers and lecturers also act as counsellors, advising on non-educational matters. Do not confuse 'counsellor' with 'counsel' (a barrister) or 'councillor' (a member of a council).

This report was prepared for the court before Anthony's case was heard. Note the framework on which any report is built.

### HEADING OF REPORT

**Re. Subject**
  Introduction
  Reason for report

**Sub-heading**
  The body of the report

  Conclusion and
  Recommendations

Name
Date

As you read the following extracts from this formal report, consider the questions in the margin.

Counsellor's Confidential Report

Re : Mr and Mrs William Mitchell

When did her husband hit her?

What caused the argument?

What happened before he was charged?

Prior to Mr and Mrs Mitchell's visit to the counsellor, Mrs Mitchell had been assaulted by her husband. This had occurred during a violent argument which had originally begun when their son requested permission to borrow their car. The attack was witnessed by the son, Anthony. Later that day, Anthony was charged with a shoplifting offence.

Now the reason for the report is given.

What facts?

Taken into consideration by whom?

It is hoped that the following facts will be taken into consideration when Mr Anthony Mitchell comes before the Court.

The main body of the report follows.

Here is an extract from a paragraph subheaded Family Background.

How did Anthony suffer?

In this marriage there were frequent violent arguments involving physical violence as a consequence of which Anthony suffered greatly both mentally and physically during his adolescence.

These comments were made about Mr William Mitchell.

Does 'on the surface' imply that Mr Mitchell has psychological problems?

> On the surface he is a very sociable, successful
> businessman, but he is now faced with early
> retirement, he is short of money and .....

Now rewrite the first and second extracts from the Counsellor's report.
Change the formal account into an informal one by including the less formal phrases from the list below.

| Formal | Less formal equivalent |
| --- | --- |
| prior to | before |
| assaulted | attacked and hit |
| occurred | happened |
| requested permission | asked to be allowed to |
| witnessed | seen |
| a shoplifting offence | stealing goods from a shop |
| taken into consideration | thought about |

What effect does this have? Which style of writing is more likely to influence a judge?

## A3  Expanding notes

Note how the Counsellor draws attention to a difficult situation.

'W.M. needs alcohol more and more.'
'Mr Mitchell is increasingly dependent on alcohol.'

Now change the following notes in the same way.

'W.M. might lose job.'
'Mr Mitchell is ......... in danger of losing .........'
'Friends have strong influences over M.W.'

Note:   dependent on
         in danger of
         influenced by

## B1    A formal memo requesting mitigation

For many months Anthony had been depressed. He had got behind with his studies and failed his exams. He has now been told that he must leave college. Here is a formal memo in mitigation of Anthony's behaviour written by the Counsellor.

As you read the following memo, think about the questions in the margin:

(The registrar is in charge of enrolments)

Does he sympathise with the Authorities?

Who decided?

What was Anthony's attitude?

Permitted – by whom?

| From: | : | J. Carlisle | **CONFIDENTIAL** |
| To: | : | College Registrar | |
| Re: | : | Anthony Mitchell | |

I have discussed Anthony Mitchell's case with my colleagues. I fully appreciate your concern about him. Anthony has informed me of your decision that he must leave college. I understand that this is a direct result of his poor academic and attendance records.

On his behalf, I would like to appeal against that decision. Anthony was referred to me at the end of last term and has cooperated in every way possible. His performance is largely due to the conflict between his parents.

I am now confident that if Anthony is permitted to continue his studies he will achieve high academic standards. Without breaking any confidence, I wish to stress that Anthony's very difficult family circumstances should be taken into account when his case comes up for review.

## B2    Formal and informal language

Note the formality of 'I fully appreciate your concern' and the more informal 'I understand how you feel.'

'Anthony informed me of your decision.' (*formal*)
'Anthony told me that you had made up your minds.' (*informal*)

'This is a direct result of his poor academic and attendance records.' (*formal*)
'Because his work is poor and he has missed lectures.' (*informal*)

a. Which formal phrase in the memo shows that the writer thinks Anthony should be allowed to stay on at college? 'I am ..........'

b. Which formal phrase expresses the hope that the authorities will treat Anthony with sympathy in view of his unhappy family background?
'I wish ..........'

Here is the Counsellor's informal file memo summarising Anthony's situation.

Note the use of 'ought' 'should' 'must' 'have to'

This direct language is suitable for a file memo, or for when you wish to be strong and assertive. However, if you wish to create goodwill and persuade people to a certain course of action it could be considered aggressive.

**CONFIDENTIAL**

REFERENCE AJ/10
Re:      Anthony Mitchell
Date:    15th July

1.  Anthony has been asked to
    leave college June 6th.
    Have been asked to speak
    for him and persuade college
    to change their minds.

2.  A. ought to re-sit exam in
    Nov.
    must leave home
    should make new friends

3.  Fees : at present A. in debt
    College will have to wait.

    Action : Write registrar,
    ask for help/understanding

    Check lodging office
    encourage sport/societies

## B3  Making recommendations

Read the following extract from the Counsellor's letter to the Court. Select the most appropriate word to make the letter positive. Be tactful and direct but not blunt.

| Having | looked at / taken into consideration | the facts which | led up to / culminated in | the charge of shoplifting, |
|---|---|---|---|---|

| we | hope you will / want you to | be as | sympathetic / lenient | as possible in your judgement. We | know / think | that |
|---|---|---|---|---|---|---|

| Anthony | should / must | be given the | chance / opportunity | to resit his examinations and continue his studies. |
|---|---|---|---|---|

| It would be | great / much appreciated | if Anthony could be | let off / discharged | and | allowed / enabled | to make a new start. |
|---|---|---|---|---|---|---|

## C1   Talking about statistics

According to the graph below it is evident that shoplifting offences have almost doubled in the past ten years. The graph shows that the number of convictions reached a peak of 81,000 last year.

After the introduction of tighter security measures five years ago, the upward trend was halted; convictions dropped to 54,000. However, since then, there has been a steady annual increase of around 12.5%.

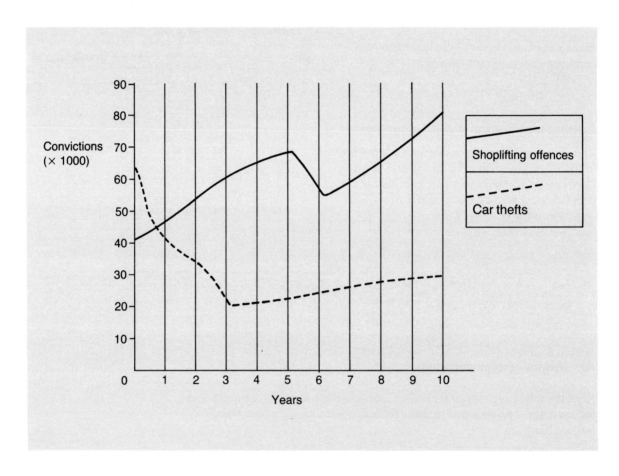

Now write a similar paragraph about the number of convictions for stealing cars over the same period. Make suitable changes in the text by referring to the dotted line on the graph. Here are some of the phrases you will need:

> according to the graph above ......
> almost halved
> was at its lowest seven years ago
> lighter penalties
> downward
> rose steadily to 28,000
> this reflects an annual increase of nearly 6%

## C2   Language for interpreting a graph

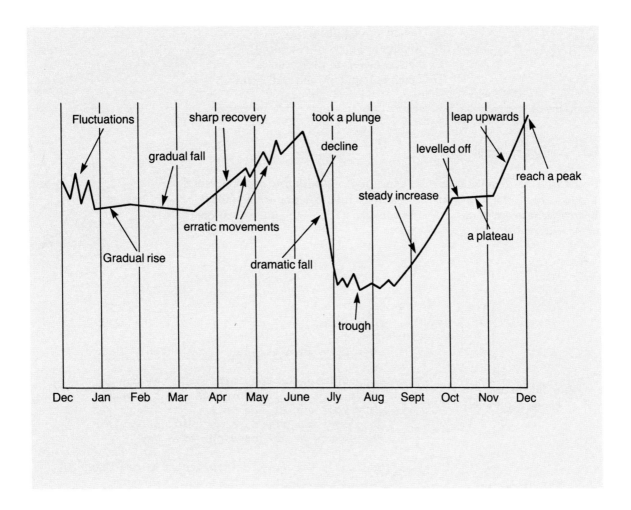

## C3

Complete the following commentary on the graph above. All the gaps can be filled with words on the graph. You may need to change some nouns into verbs.

From December to January, while sales were erratic, prices ....(1).... Prices ....(2).... in January but the ....(3)....
was not maintained. There was a .........(4)......... in February and early March. In mid-March they made a
.........(5).......... Throughout May and June movements were ....(6).... A ....(7).... occurred in late June but the
downward trend was halted in early July. Throughout July and early August they remained in a ....(8)....
They started to recover in August and by September the .........(9)......... was maintained until the second week
in October. Prices .........(10)...... during October and remained on a .........(11)......... until November when they
....(12).... Prices reached a .........(13)......... in December.

In this Unit you will find:

**A.** Letters of complaint
**B.** Replies to letters of complaint
**C.** Letters giving an ultimatum
**D.** Letters of apology and settlement

## A1   A letter of complaint

Read this letter. Bente Rasmussen, Director of a Danish firm of spinners and weavers, hired a car for her marketing trip to Eire. After returning the car, Bente Rasmussen sent this letter. As you read it, think about the questions in the margin.

Dear Sirs,

<u>Car Hire Invoice 7430 - April 7th - 12th</u>

*Who did she want to contact and why?*

I am writing to complain about the car I hired from you on the above dates.  When I left your car at Dublin Airport, there was no one at the depot so I could not explain the events of the previous five days.

*Why did she drive carefully?*

On Sunday 7th April, I collected a car from your depot at the Airport.  A few hours later, the car overheated and had to be replaced.  The next day, the transmission became very noisy.  After repeated unsuccessful attempts to contact you, I had to ask a local garage to inspect it.  I enclose the garage's invoice for £35.35.

*Who assured her? Which day was that?*

On the Wednesday, I telephoned you in Dublin and was asked to take the car to your agent in Cork.  The car was checked and I was assured that it was roadworthy.  However, the next day the car pulled violently to the right, narrowly missing a stone wall.  I could not see anything wrong so I continued carefully to a garage in Limerick.  I telephoned your office for advice, but all I could get was the answer-phone.  I left

*What details?*

details, asking you to phone me back.

| | Having heard nothing by 6 p.m., I asked the garage to repair the car so that I could get back to Dublin. They did so. I enclose the garage bill £84.50. |
|---|---|
| What did they do? | |

I returned the car as arranged on Friday at 7 p.m. but your office was already closed and I saw no one.

<table>
<tr><td>What frustration?</td><td>I am sure you will appreciate the annoyance and frustration of the past week during which I know I have lost substantial business. I look forward to receiving your comments and to receiving your cheque for £119.85 in settlement for the two repair bills.</td></tr>
<tr><td>How did Bente arrive at the sum of £119.85?</td><td></td></tr>
</table>

Yours faithfully,

*Bente Rasmussen.*

Bente Rasmussen

Enclosures. 2

---

Notice the basic principles of writing a letter of complaint:

> Be polite.
> State clearly and factually what is wrong.
> Support your claim with documents.
> Imply that your claim will be met as a matter of course.
> Summarise your claim. State clearly what you expect.
> Decide on the emphasis you want to give.
> Do you want to appear threatening, pleading, reasoning or reproaching?

Notice the phrases Bente used to express her complaint:

> 'I am writing to complain about ......'
> 'I am sure you will appreciate the annoyance ......'

and for ending her letter:

> 'I look forward *to hearing* your comments.
>                 *to receiving* your cheque.

Note another way of expressing the following:
> 'I tried many times to contact you, but I had no success, so eventually I ......'
> ★ 'After repeated unsuccessful attempts to contact you I eventually ......'

Now do the same with:

(a)  'Very often he tried to put forward new ideas, but without success so eventually he resigned.'
'After ...................'

'I heard nothing by 6 pm so I asked the garage to fix the car.'
★ 'Having heard nothing by 6 pm, I asked the garage to fix the car.'

Now you do the same with the following:

(b)  'I left the car at the depot, then I caught the plane to Copenhagen.'
'Having ...................'

(c)  'I spoke to the Company Secretary, and decided to write to you.'
'Having ...................'

61

## A2  Polite complaint and strong accusation

Your first letter of complaint should sound calm and reasonable. You will probably get better and quicker service than if you demand, threaten or accuse.

Compare these sentences:
    'There was no one at the depot.'
is not as accusing as:
    'You had closed your depot.'

    'I was told the car was roadworthy.'
is not as accusing as:
    'You told me the car was roadworthy.'

The first sentence in each case is indirect –
'There was no one.' 'I was told.'
The second sentence is direct – 'You had closed.' 'You told me.'

(i)  Now make these sentences more polite:

    a.  You delayed me. (I was ......)
    b.  You assured me that everything was alright. (I was ..................)
    c.  You gave me the wrong car. (I was ..................)
    d.  You made a mistake. (A mistake ..................)
    e.  You have caused me a lot of frustration. (I have ..................)

(ii)  Note the aggressive tone of the following. It comes from a letter of complaint to a neighbour.

    I must inform you that I have a number of complaints to make about recent events. Firstly, there is the problem of parking your vehicles. You must be aware that .......

Change the above extract and make it more diplomatic. You wish to cause the minimum offence to your neighbour.

Choose one of these words and phrases to fill each gap.
a.  few weeks
b.  like to make
c.  sorry
d.  one or two points
e.  question of
f.  write
g.  look at

I am ....(1).... to have to ....(2).. but there are ...(3)... I would ...(4)... about the past ...(5)... First of all can we ....(6)... the ...(7)... parking your cars. Did you know that ...................

If you wish to modify your complaint avoid words which have strong negative associations. A positive or tactful word compared with a negative one might help to create goodwill.

| Positive | Negative |
| --- | --- |
| incorrect | wrong |
| misunderstanding | mistake |
| imperfect | faulty |
| ineffective | useless |

Compare these ways of saying something.
    We received your criticisms. (*negative*)
★ Thank you for your comments. (*positive*)

    Your order will be three weeks late. (*negative*)
★ We have been obliged to reschedule your order. (*positive*)

## A3   Exercise: Letter of complaint

Here is an extract from a letter of complaint from a manufacturer to his
supplier.
(i)  Choose the correct word from the margin to fill the gaps.

<table>
<tr><td>

could<br>
original<br>
emphasise<br>
on inspection<br>
replacement<br>
particular<br>
be grateful<br>
delays

</td><td>

**Invoice AJ 610 (curtain fabric)**

Thank you for your consignment 2021 which
arrived yesterday. Unfortunately .....(1) we find
that Quality 402 on the invoice is several
shades lighter than the .....(2) sample. We must
.....(3) that this .....(4) quality is required
urgently if we are to meet our production
commitments.
We would .....(5) if you .....(6) let us have an
immediate .....(7) from stock.

</td></tr>
</table>

(ii)  When you have filled in the gaps in the following extract, read it again
and decide how *you* would feel if *you* received such a letter.

<table>
<tr><td>

prepared<br>
trouble<br>
persuaded<br>
appreciate<br>
defective<br>
purchase<br>
adjustment<br>
under guarantee<br>
still

</td><td>

I was .....(1) by your agent to .....(2) the XL 150
sewing machine. I regret to inform you that I
have had nothing but .....(3) with it ever since.
As it was .....(4) I returned it to your agent on
two occasions for .....(5) but unfortunately it is
.....(6) unserviceable. I am afraid the machine is
.....(7) and I am not .....(8) to have it repaired a
third time. I would very much .....(9) a
replacement without delay.

I look forward to hearing from you by return.

</td></tr>
</table>

Do you feel the writer is justified in his request? Would you make every
effort to help him? He is angry, but note how he tries to soften his
accusation by using these phrases.

    I regret ......
    Unfortunately ......
    I am afraid ......

Notice how he uses these phrases to sound very firm.
    I have had nothing but trouble ......
    ...... it is still unserviceable.
    I am not prepared to ......

## B1    A reply to a letter of complaint

Read this letter of apology from Mr O'Callaghan to Bente Rasmussen's letter of complaint. As you read it consider the questions in the margin.

What was due to the technical inspection?

What had happened to the wheel-bearing?

In what condition?

Who paid £430.00?

What do they feel Bente should have done?

What are they implying?

How generous are they being?

Why not?

What is their solution?

Dear Ms. Rasmussen

### Car Hire Invoice 7430

Firstly, we would like to apologise sincerely for the delay in replying to your letter of April 15th. This was due to the technical inspection which was necessary before we could give you a satisfactory answer.

As soon as we learnt of the problem with the vehicle, we arranged for it to be collected by the main agents for Dublin and asked them for a detailed report. They found that the offside rear wheel-bearing had gone, and due to the car having been driven in this condition, the differential gear was badly worn and needed replacing. The total cost of this was £430. If you had taken the car off the road at the first sign of trouble, it would only have cost us £150. Therefore, the fact that you continued to drive the car has cost us an additional £280. In the normal way, we would have been obliged to debit you with this excess repair bill. However, in view of the inconvenience you suffered, we are prepared to waive our claim on you.

We sympathise with you and deeply regret the difficulties you experienced. However, we regret that in no way can we be held responsible for any costs you incurred. We would ask you to refer to Clause 14 of the Hire Agreement. We hope that now you know the full facts of the case you will withdraw your claim and accept our solution.

Yours sincerely,

D. O'Callaghan

DECLAN O'CALLAGHAN

When dealing with complaints the first rule is to respond quickly. The correspondent needs to know the complaint has been received and is being dealt with.

Even if you feel the complaint is not justified, the following principles
should be observed when replying. Notice how Mr O'Callaghan observes
these principles in his letter.

> Acknowledge and apologise.
> Give your version of the facts.
> Explain what action is being taken.
> Concede a point if possible.
> Sympathise and reassure your correspondent.

Note the following language which can be used in answering complaints.

Apologising and excusing.

> We are sorry to hear ......
> We were distressed to learn/hear about ......
> We must apologise for the delay in returning/replying/forwarding ......
> The delay was due to the fact that/the result of ......
> I would like to explain the situation.

Making concessions.

> In the normal way we would have been obliged to ......
> However, in view of the circumstances ......
> Under the circumstances we are prepared to/can ......

Disclaiming responsibility.

> We regret that in no way can we be held responsible for ......
> We would like to emphasise that it is your responsibility to ......
> Now that you know the full facts perhaps you ......
> Now that you understand the situation perhaps you ......
> We are bound by the terms of our contract ......
> If you check, you will find that the guarantee states ......

## B2   Formal and informal language

You must decide which approach is most suitable in your circumstances.

A close friend would be surprised to receive this apology.

> 'I very much regret the inconvenience my action may have caused you. Please accept my sincere
> apologies.'

A customer who is a complete stranger would be equally surprised to receive his apology.

> 'I'm sorry for the bother you've had. I hope it hasn't upset you too much.'

Note the use of contractions: 'I'm', 'you've', 'hasn't'. These appear more and more frequently in letters
today once a relationship has been established.

Make the following sentences less formal:

(a) Under no circumstances can we extend your credit.
    We are sorry ............... unable ............... .

(b) I appreciate the honour of being asked to address your members but I regret ............... .
    Thank ............... invitation to speak. ............... sorry ............... .

(c) You would be well advised to contact your local representative.
    I ............... suggest ............... get in touch with ............... .

## B3    Responding to letters of complaint

In section **A3** you were asked to complete letters of complaint. Now reply to those letters.
Fill in the gaps, choosing the appropriate word from the margin.

(i) A Telex

REGRET
EITHER
STANDS
SINCERE
ALLOWANCE
SUGGEST
OR
PRODUCTION

```
RE QUALITY 402

.....(1).. APOLOGIES FOR DISCREPANCY. .....(2).. TWO

ALTERNATIVES ......(3).. RETURN GOODS FOR FREE

RE-DYEING .....(4).. MAKE UP CLOTH AS IT ......(5).. WE COULD

OFFER 30% ......(6).. .....(7).. QUALITY 402 NOW OUT OF ......(8)..

LETTER FOLLOWS.

BEST REGARDS.
```

(ii) A letter

Complete the letter using appropriate phrases from the left hand margin.

suit your convenience
find it satisfactory
very sorry to hear
sent to you
have arranged for
are certain
apologise sincerely
contact you

```
We were .....(1)..... of your problems with our

sewing machine XL 150. We .....(2)..... our local

representative to collect it. He will .....(3).....

and arrange a date to .....(4)..... A replacement

machine will be .....(5)..... within the next five

days. We .....(6)..... that you will .....(7).....

in every way.

Once again we .....(8)..... for any inconvenience

we might have caused.
```

## C1  A strongly worded complaint

Here is Bente Rasmussen's letter in response to the one she received from
Mr O'Callaghan.

Dear Mr O'Callaghan,

I was astonished to receive your letter of
15th April. I would have thought that a
reputable company such as yours would have
accepted, not denied, your responsibilities.

I must repeat, the problems I experienced
with your car were due to your negligence,
not mine. In view of the business I have
lost, not to mention the anxiety and
discomfort, I consider my request for a
refund of your repair bill very reasonable.

I would like to hear from you by return of
post, but must point out that unless you
settle my claim in full you leave me no
alternative but to place the matter in the
hands of my solicitors.

Yours truly,

*Bente Rasmussen.*

Bente Rasmussen

Notice how Bente expresses her emotions in her first sentence.

'I was astonished to .....................'

Here are some other ways she could have expressed her anger in a formal
way.

| | | |
|---|---|---|
| I am | somewhat<br>very | disappointed ...... |
| I was | most<br>extremely | concerned ......<br>surprised ...... |

And here are some extreme words.

I am/was | disgusted ......
| furious ......
| outraged ......

And if she had wished to be more moderate about her feelings she might
have written:

I am/ was | hurt ..........
| upset ..........
| sad ......
| confused ......
| surprised ......

Notice how she rejects Mr O'Callaghan's arguments.

'I would have thought that a company such as yours would have
accepted, not denied, ......'
'...... I consider that my request ...... is reasonable.'

Notice also how she puts the blame on Mr O'Callaghan.

'Not only did you ...... but you ......'

And how she makes a polite but direct request:

'I would like to hear from you by return of post.'

## C2 A strongly worded complaint

Mr O'Callaghan did not reply by return of post. After waiting two weeks,
Bente wrote the following letter.

Dear Mr O'Callaghan,

As you have not replied to my letter of
April 22nd, I am now left with no
alternative but to start proceedings
against you. I intend to claim all the
expenses I incurred on your behalf, also
for the loss of business and any legal
costs.

I hereby inform you that I am lodging a
formal complaint with your company's Trade
Association. I have no doubt that the
matter will be of considerable interest to
them. Copies of our correspondence will
be sent to a popular motoring magazine.
The editor, who is a personal friend, will
ensure that the matter will receive maximum
publicity.

Yours truly,

*Bente Rasmussen.*

Bente Rasmussen

Notice how Bente gives an ultimatum.

> 'I am now left with no alternative
> but to ..................'

Here are some other phrases.

> 'You leave me no option but to ......'
> 'I am forced to/obliged to ......'
> 'Unless you ...... I will ......'

Notice how Bente explains what action she will take. She will do three things.

> She is going to lodge a complaint.
>
> She will send copies of their correspondence to the editor.
>
> She will see that it is published.

Notice how Bente says what action she will take.

'**Not only am I** lodging a complaint, *but also* I am sending copies of our correspondence to the Editor *and I will see* that it is published.'

Now write similar sentences using the same structure with the following information:

(a) return faulty goods
cancel further orders
transfer business to another supplier

'Not only am I .........., but also ......... and I will transfer ...................'

(b) employ more staff
enter new markets
increase our advertising budget

'Not only are we ................... We are also ................... increase ...................'

## D1   Letters of apology and settlement

When the relationship between two parties becomes severely strained, as in this case, only a most polite and conciliatory letter can restore goodwill.

The car hire firm values its good reputation. It does not want adverse publicity. As soon as the threatening letter arrived, one of the Directors telephoned Bente immediately. He explained that a letter was on its way to Denmark and it had crossed Bente's letter.

The firm had already decided that they must meet Bente's claim in order to preserve the Company's good name. In the letter of apology you will see 15 blank spaces. Below are 15 words or phrases. The first of each pair is slightly less formal than the second.

### Words and Phrases

| | |
|---|---|
| off sick | suddenly taken ill |
| accidentally | inadvertently |
| thought | consideration |
| really upset | most concerned |
| excuse us | accept our apologies |
| too much | unreasonable |
| thinking it over | re-considering the circumstances |
| position | situation |
| we are happy to enclose | we have pleasure in enclosing |
| stick to | comply with |
| faulty | defective |
| thoughtlessly | negligently |
| word | assurance |
| unsafe | unroadworthy |
| give us the chance | allow us the opportunity |

a. Decide where the pairs should go (e.g. 1 – most concerned).
b. Now decide whether at each point the less formal or the more formal should be used.

Dear Ms. Rasmussen,

We were ...(1)... to receive your letter of May 10th and have given it careful ..(2).. Please ..(3).. for the delay in replying. I must explain that Mr. O'Callaghan was ..(4)..., and your letter was ..(5)... put on one side. I have been asked to take over where he left off.

On ..(6)... we do realise that you were placed in a difficult ..(7).. We appreciate that you felt it would have been ..(8)... to expect you to ..(9)... the fine print on the contract. Therefore, ..(10).. our cheque for £115.93. We would not like you to think however, that we ..(11).. send our customers out in ..(12).. cars. On checking with the main agents of Apollo, they confirm that the ..(13).. wheel-bearing could not have been discovered without stripping the rear axle. You have our ..(14).. that the misfortunes of your trip were quite exceptional. We hope that one day you will return to Ireland and ..(15).. to prove this to you.

Yours sincerely,

*David Green*

David Green
Director

Note that 'the fine print' is the legal detail in the contract, usually printed in small type.

## D2 Letter of Reconciliation

Having received the apology, Bente decides to end this matter with a
short letter of reconciliation, reckoning that in business an ally is always
useful. She may, after all, want to use the firm again.

Read the following letter.

Dear Mr. Green,

    Thank you for your letter and the enclosed cheque.

    I am glad that the matter had to go no further, and
am sorry the delay was caused by illness. If I need to
hire a car during my next trip I hope I may call on your
services again. You may be interested to know that,
despite the lost opportunities, my last visit eventually
proved quite successful.

    Yours sincerely,

*Bente Rasmussen.*

Bente Rasmussen

Now write a short letter of reconciliation in response to the letter of
settlement in B3.

# UNIT 8

In this Unit you will find:

**A.** Letters of application for a grant
**B.** A curriculum vitae and application form
**C.** Letters of reference and interview assessments

## A1 An advertisement for a grant

Read this advertisement for a grant carefully. Think about the questions in the margin as you read.

Is Sara Jensén still alive?

To what end?

Who has to approve of the project?

What 2 things must candidates do?

### The Sara Jensen Memorial Award

#### Founded 1978

This award was established to encourage successfully established women to use their skills and experience in fields other than their own. To this end, financial assistance will be given to selected candidates for a period of one year. Substantial grants will enable successful candidates to live and work in another country. They will be able to work on a project of their own choice. The project will be subject to selectors' approval. Candidates should explain why they consider they would be eligible for a grant and how they would use it. If you are interested, please write to Ann Ridley.

When applying for any post or grant, make sure you:

    – read the advertisement carefully
    – analyse the wording
    – establish exactly what is required

Re-write the advertisement in your own words. Make it shorter; take out at least 50 words. The following must not be left out.

    – grants for women             – candidates must submit details
    – live and work in another country    – how would they spend the grant
    – choose a project

73

## A2   A letter of application

Wanjuki Mungi, one of the candidates, completed an application form and drew up her curriculum vitae.
Here is part of her covering letter accompanying the application.
Read it carefully and note the comments on the structure of the letter in the margin.

CONFIDENTIAL

Dear Ms. Ridley,

Introduction

Thank you for sending me an application form
which I now enclose, together with my
curriculum vitae.

Motivation

Aims

If my application were successful, I should
like to return to Africa to fulfil a
personal ambition. I wish to become involved
in the establishment of craft training
workshops and community care centres. I feel
strongly that local personnel must be trained
who will eventually be able to administer the
projects.

Qualifications

I feel I am well qualified to carry out such
a programme for the following reasons:

Experience

1.  As a business woman who has worked in
    many capacities in a highly competitive
    field, my experience would be invaluable
    in fund-raising and in the development
    of community projects.

2.  My particular interest is in helping the
    adolescent to acquire useful skills.
    Through local community work, I am well
    aware of the adolescent's problems and
    difficulties.

3.  By living and working in the community,
    I would be able to help in the
    development of trades and crafts, which
    would eventually produce profits to be
    re-invested in the local community.

74

The person who reads your letter of application will look for evidence of your motivation, expectations (aims), work experience and calibre based on your experience and your potential.

Note how Wanjuki expresses her motivation and expectations.

> 'If my application were successful, I should like to return to Africa.'
> 'I wish to become involved in ......'
> 'I feel strongly that ......'

Notice how she gives evidence of her work experience.

> 'I feel I am well qualified to ...... for the following reasons.'
> 'As a ...... who has ......, my experience would be invaluable in ......'
> 'My particular interest is ......'
> 'Through ...... I am well aware of ......'
> 'By ...... ing and ...... ing I would be able to ......'

Wanjuki concludes her letter with personal details.

```
In the past, family commitments and the
fact that my capital is tied up in my
business have prevented me from taking
action. However, circumstances have changed.
I am now a free agent. I should be very
pleased to attend an interview and discuss
the grant in more detail. I look forward
to hearing from you.
```

Wanjuki does not go into detail about her family situation. She states:

> 'In the past, family commitments have prevented me ......'

She does not explain here in detail what the commitments are.
She adopts a positive approach.

> 'However, circumstances have changed. I am now a free agent.'

Once again there is no need to go into detail about the 'circumstances'.

Other ways of ending a letter of application are:

> I have no urgent commitments at present.
> I am available; should you wish to discuss matters further, please contact me at ......
> I would welcome the opportunity to meet you.
> You can contact me on 01-246-8041 between 9 am and 5 pm at the above address.

## A3    Job requirements

Here is a list of requirements for different jobs.

Use your dictionary to check any words you are doubtful about.

| *to be* | *to have* |
|---|---|
| sociable | appropriate professional qualifications |
| numerate | sound practical experience* |
| aggressive | integrity |
| mature | talent |
| self-motivated | the ability to establish rapport |
| conscientious | drive |
| dedicated | a proven track record* |
| patient | stamina |
| bright | flair |
| | aptitude for ...... |
| | industrial experience |

* 'Sound experience' is experience based on a good foundation and a 'proven track record' is an established record of success behind you.

Choose five requirements from the above list for each of the following people and place them in order of priority:

| Order of priority | a sales executive | a concert pianist | a brain surgeon | a teacher |
|---|---|---|---|---|
| Essential<br>Important<br>Preferable<br>Irrelevant | | | | |

Now look at the following three job advertisements.

We are looking for a junior audio-typist to join the busy general office of our local drapery firm. A good typing speed is essential, and a knowledge of shorthand would be an advantage. If you are cheerful and get on with people, why not write for an application form.

**A.2. Personnel Recruitment**
**Marketing Manager**
**£20 K + p.a.**

Our client, a rapidly expanding company in the field of home electrical appliances, wishes to appoint a Marketing Manager. This is a senior appointment, and success as reflected by growth in market share could well open the door of the boardroom. A salary in excess of £20,000 per year and usual benefits including car and profit share are offered in exchange for a proven track record and dynamic approach to product innovation.

**Castings and Foundries Ltd.**

**The company** A small firm making specialised machine tools for the automotive industry.

**The post** Personnel Manager, responsible for all aspects of employee relations, including recruitment and training. Must have experience of salary negotiations with recognised trade unions.

**The challenge** Due to restructuring, the company was recently forced to revise downward its employee requirements. The postholder will be expected to assume considerable responsibility for the smooth running of the personnel operation.

Using these as a model, write similar advertisements for the following vacancies.

(i)  Clerk: large furniture store. Must know book keeping and accounts. Ideally should have experience with computerised ledger systems but this is not vital. Orderly mind is an asset; somebody who is methodical. Work is routine but exacting as small mistakes are hard to correct.

(ii)  Export Manager for small electronics firm anxious to break into the American market.

(iii)  Medical advisor to medium size industrial company; new factory process involves use of asbestos. Responsible for positive staff attitude to health and safety at work. Must be fully aware of all legislation.

## B1  A curriculum vitae (a C.V.)

Your C.V. is probably one of the most important documents you will ever produce. If you have to apply for many different positions, it is advisable to draw up a standard C.V. to send with your letter of application.

Your curriculum vitae is your personal sales letter. It should be:
  a. easy to read
  b. well laid out
  c. comprehensive
  d. written in note form
  e. arranged under headings and sub-headings

Some employers find it useful if you start with details of your present professional experience and work backwards.

On the next page you will find the C.V. which Wanjuki drew up for the selectors of the Sara Jensen award.

## B2  Presenting a C.V.

As you read the C.V. choose from the words in the left hand margin to fill the gaps.

```
                        CURRICULUM VITAE

                             Wanjuki Mungi
                             18 Gomm Road
                             London
                             Telephone : 01-246-0021
```

liaising
overall
purchased
responsible
exceeded
trained
devised
turnover
strategies

negotiated
supervised
received
specialising
appreciation

```
A proprietor of five jewellery/textile boutiques

with experience in buying, marketing and

designing.


Professional experience:

1970 - present day : Proprietor of Wanjuki

Jewels.

Five retail outlets specialising in fashion

jewellery and textiles. ..(1).. responsibility

including financial and budgetary control, staff

welfare (53) buying, marketing, designing and

..(2).... with suppliers. ..(3).. for collection

buying ..(4).. a boutique in partnership and built

up a chain of boutiques over eight years.

Increased ..(5).. and profits.

Recruited and ..(6).. all sales staff.

..(7).. and implemented marketing ..(8)..

Achieved and ..(9).. targets.

1968/70 Assistant Manager with Charmain Textiles

Manufacturing Company. ..(10).. 15 staff with
```

special responsibility for budgetary control and financial accounting for three outlets. Successfully .....(11) contracts with Continental, African and Asian textile suppliers.

1966/68  Sales Assistant with James Fashions, a company .....(12) in fashion jewellery and cosmetics.
.....(13) sound basic training in all aspects of selling, buying and design .....(14)


| | |
|---|---|
| Education: | The Convent, Mombasa 1952-1956 |
| | Exams : General Certificate of Education 8 subjects |
| Languages : | English (fluent) Masai (mother tongue) |
| | Swahili (fluent) French (working knowledge) |
| Interests : | Family life and working on community projects in E. London. |
| | Vice-chairman Resettlement Project |
| Personal : | Age 43. Widow. 4 grown-up children. |
| | Enjoy reading, painting, designing, debating |

If you have had limited business experience, it may be necessary to give a detailed account of schooling and further education. List your accomplishments under suitable headings, such as:

    Qualifications
    Courses attended
    Examinations taken
    Degrees obtained

## B3 Completing an application form

All the information you need to complete this form has been given to you in
**B2**. Complete sections 1, 2, 5, 6, 7, 8, 10, 11.

---

APPLICATION FORM                                    Date.....................................

### *Sara Jensen Memorial Trust Fund*

**CONFIDENTIAL**
Use BLOCK letters throughout please

| (1) SURNAME | OTHER NAMES | DATE OF BIRTH |
|---|---|---|
| | | 12.12.1940 |

| (2) ADDRESS (PERMANENT) (TEMPORARY) | EDUCATION (3) St Anns Convent Mombasa, Kenya. E. Africa. | PLACE Nairobi, Kenya |

NATIONALITY at birth KENYAN
Now BRITISH

MARITAL STATUS (5)
(delete as necessary)

Single
Married
Separated
Divorced
Widowed

TELEPHONE
Home
Business

LANGUAGES SPOKEN (6)
(degree of fluency)

(4) ANY SERIOUS ILLNESSES

(8) SYNOPSIS OF YOUR CAREER

DEPENDENTS (give age if under 18)
(7)

(9) STATE THE MOST SIGNIFICANT FEATURES WHICH HAVE INFLUENCED YOUR CAREER   In 1943 FATHER
died. Mother left village to become successful trader in textiles. Travelled throughout Sudan and
Africa. When my husband died in 1966 I had to support three young children.

(10) REASONS FOR APPLYING FOR GRANT

(11) SPARE TIME INTERESTS

Please supply the names, addresses and telephone numbers of three referees in the space provided overleaf.

80

## C1 Writing a reference

Always ask someone before you give their name as reference.
When employees leave a company, they may ask for a testimonial or 'open letter of reference' to take with them.
Here is the open reference Wanjuki received when she left Charmain Textiles:

```
                    To Whom It May Concern


Wanjuki Mungi was employed by Charmain Textiles
from Jan. 1968-Nov. 1970.  Throughout her time
with the organisation she was a most valuable
employee and colleague.

Wanjuki has a logical mind, is sensitive and
is an effective motivator.  She created strong
personal relationships in day-to-day contacts
with top designers, and initiated positive
action in others through full and active
membership of the management team.

Charmain Textiles will always be happy to
re-employ her and wish her every success with
her new venture.




F. Hutchinson
General Manager        November 22nd 1970
```

## C2 Choosing the 'correct' adjective

Two interviewers were asked their opinion of Wanjuki's project.

Interviewer A, a young optimistic person who saw the project as 'ambitious but expensive', used the words in list **1**.

Interviewer B, an older, more critical and pessimistic person, who saw the project as 'impracticable and extravagant', used the words in list **2**.

Although the words may have approximately the same meaning they can convey different implications. Look up these words in your dictionary if you are not sure of their meanings.

| **1** | **2** |
|---|---|
| sensitive | nervous |
| confident | aggressive |
| specialised | limited |
| articulate | talkative |
| reserved | anti-social |
| economical | mean |

## C3 Interview assessment form

Read the 'Points to Check' on the extract taken from the assessment form below. This was completed by the selectors after they interviewed Wanjuki.

| POINTS TO CHECK | | COMMENTS |
|---|---|---|
| 1. Education<br><br>   a. exceeds requirements<br>   b. meets requirements<br>   c. does not meet requirements | ☐<br>☐<br>☐ | |

Now refer to the adjectives in **C2** and decide which adjective would refer to Sections 1–6. Complete the assessment form. Fill in Interviewer A's comments about Wanjuki and place a ( ✓ ) in the appropriate box.

For example: Interviewer A would consider Wanjuki's education specialised or that it exceeds requirements but B would consider it does *not* meet requirements and it was limited.

| POINTS TO CHECK | | COMMENTS |
|---|---|---|
| 1. Education<br><br>   a. exceeds requirements<br>   b. meets requirements<br>   c. does not meet requirements | ☐<br>☑<br>☐ | *Specialised* |
| 2. Attitude to money<br><br>   a. all important<br>   b. a consideration<br>   c. unimportant | ☐<br>☐<br>☐ | |
| 3. Assertiveness<br><br>   a. forceful<br>   b. assured<br>   c. mild | ☐<br>☐<br>☐ | |
| 4. Ability to take criticism<br>   a. able<br>   b. fairly able<br>   c. not able | ☐<br>☐<br>☐ | |
| 5. Sociability<br><br>   a. wide circle of friends<br>   b. more sociable than reserved<br>   c. more reserved than sociable | ☐<br>☐<br>☐ | |
| 6. Speech<br>   a. good speaker<br>   b. reasonable speaker<br>   c. rather poor speaker | ☐<br>☐<br>☐ | |

## C4  Language for writing a reference

Notice how to give praise:

'She has been a most
| valuable employee' |
|---|
| loyal' |
| hardworking' |
| co-operative' |

'She has a logical mind and *is* sensitive'

'She has a talent/flair for design and is creative'

*Note:* Wanjuki was well able to motivate people:
★ 'She is an effective motivator'

Change the following the same way:
  (i) Wanjuki was well able to lead others
      She ...................
 (ii) Wanjuki was well able to administer the office:
      She ...................
(iii) Wanjuki was well able to design
      She ...................
(iv) Wanjuki was well able to manage people
      She ...................

'She was a very active member of the management team and she had a good relationship with colleagues.'

Note how this can be said in another way:
★ Through full and active membership of the management team

| she | created |  |
|---|---|---|
| | initiated | |
| | inspired | strong personal relationships |
| | encouraged | |
| | built up | |

After her interview, Wanjuki was told that she had been put on the short list. This can also be expressed:
    'Wanjuki was shortlisted'
Do *you* think she should get an award?

Write a reference for a good friend who you think should be shortlisted for such an award.

# UNIT 9

In this Unit you will find:

**A.** A standard direct mail letter (hard sell)
**B.** A standard direct mail letter (soft sell) and reply to an enquiry
**C.** An advertising brochure

### A1 Composing a letter using a word processor

When texts have to be revised, re-arranged, added to or changed in any way, a word processor is invaluable. The machine's flexibility makes it ideal for those who compose directly on to a typewriter. However, special language skills are needed in order to use the machine effectively. No matter how sophisticated the machine, a sound knowledge of grammar, punctuation, spelling and composition is needed. Insertions or amendments are made to the 'building blocks' or between blocks to make the letter more personal or more appropriate. If this is not done skilfully, the result can be a clumsy, disjointed text, difficult to read.

This Unit has been designed to help you with this particular skill. It also exposes you to some examples of the American style of writing, which differs from British English not just in tone but, sometimes, in vocabulary and spelling. Here are some of the American English words and phrases in this Unit, with their British English equivalent.

| American | British |
|---|---|
| February thru' (= through) March | February to March |
| Executive Vice-President | Managing Director |
| fiber | fibre |
| fabricating | making |
| gasoline | petrol |
| corporation | company |

In a book this size, it is impossible to illustrate the differences between English and American English. The BBC English by Television Video Course 'Follow me to San Francisco' is recommended for those students who wish to make a more detailed study of American style. In this Unit, material which originated in the United States has been written with American spelling.

### A2 A 'hard sell' approach

A company in America bought 2000 names from a list-broker in Europe (a list-broker sells lists of names of people or companies which have some connection with each other). Here is the letter which was drafted to send out as a mail shot.

85

Read the letter carefully and note the comments on the structure of the letter in the margin.

Dear Mr ....,

**Introduction – note the emphatic, reassuring tone.**

We believe that your company, as a progressive organisation, will be interested in the possibility of acquiring businesses in the United States. Our corporation is recognised as one of the leaders in the field of company restructuring.

**Who they are**
**What they do**

**Background – past achievements**
**Detail**

We are not brokers. We work full time for our clients in return for retainer fees. Over the past twenty-five years we have worked with a number of major North American and European companies on a confidential basis. Our headquarters is in Brussels. We have offices in Washington, San Francisco and Vancouver. Our methods are advanced, effective and practical.

**Object of the letter**

**How the recipient will profit**

**Proposal**

Frankly, Mr ....., we would very much like to have your company as a client. We are certain we can help your company to develop and expand here in the States. As President, I have approached a selected group of highly successful, non-conflicting corporations in Europe. I most sincerely believe that there are unusually profitable opportunities for your organisation in the United States at this particular time.

If this idea interests you, we can prepare a general proposal with no obligation on your part whatsoever. When you have read the detailed proposal, we could arrange a meeting.

**Action expected from recipient**

Would you be good enough to write to me. I am most interested to hear your comments and look forward to hearing from you.

**American closing phrase**

Very truly yours,

J. Earle King, President

In this standard letter, the writer attempts to attract the reader's attention in the first paragraph and make him want to read further. The writer uses positive words and makes definite statements.

'We *believe* that your company, as a progressive organisation, *will* be interested ......'
'...... our corporation is recognised as one of the leaders in the field of company restructuring.'

Once the reader's attention has been caught, the writer continues with his message. Note how the reader is reassured both by the disclaimer and by the strong positive words.

> 'We are not ....... We work .......'
> 'Our methods are *advanced*, *effective* and *practical*.'

The writer tries to convey the impression that he is writing to an individual and not to just a name on a mailing list. This is common practice today, but more and more people recognise the insincerity of such an approach.

> 'Frankly, Mr ......'

The writer tries to impress and flatter the reader.

> 'As President, I have approached a selected group of highly successful ......'

He implies that he is already on good terms by changing from the impersonal 'we' to the personal 'I'.

> '*I* have approached ......'
> '*I* most sincerely believe ......'
> '*I* am most interested to hear ......'

The 'hard sell' approach in standard letters may have an adverse effect on some readers. The letter is in danger of being thrown straight into the waste-paper basket.

## A3  Modifying a standard letter

(i) Frequently, extra information has to be added to existing texts stored on floppy disk. For example, having read the first draft, the writer of the letter in A2 wanted to add these two facts:

★ The company was founded in 1959.
★ The purpose of this company is to help firms such as that of this reader.

These two facts could be included at the end of the first paragraph.

'Our corporation, which was founded in 1959 to help firms such as yours, is recognised as one of the leaders in the field of company restructuring'.

(ii) Now add the following points to the original letter found in **A2**.

a. The company is an international consulting firm of professional executives. (Background information.)
b. The professional executives have helped their clients on many occasions to expand their operations in the States. (Background information.)
c. The writer wishes to add that the general proposal would describe in detail how the programme works. (Action proposed.)

## B1 Standard paragraphs

Here are some paragraphs from a standard letter. They are not in the correct order. Complete the gaps in the following texts.
 (i) Choose from the left hand margin. The alternatives are synonymous.
(ii) Re-arrange the paragraphs to form a coherent letter to send to European companies. Refer to the letter in **A2** for the correct sequence of paragraphs.

Alternative phrases

### A. Past achievements:

liaison
close co-operation

are well aware of/fully understand

> We have worked in ..$^{(1)}$.. with companies which are accustomed to contracts in excess of a million dollars. We ..$^{(2)}$.. ..... the necessity for confidentiality. Our relationship with the companies we represent is always at Presidential level.

### B. Details of who they are, what they do:

Our clientele consists of/We represent

are able to warehouse/have facilities for warehousing.

> .....$^{(3)}$..... American companies who are primarily interested in long-term contracts for the production of complete units. We .....$^{(4)}$..... your parts and we can ship to your assigned location.

### C. Introductory comments:

We would like to draw your attention to/ You may not have heard of

Knowledge and experience/ expertise

> .....$^{(5)}$..... our organisation. We market our clients' excess capacity and we would like to offer you/our ..$^{(6)}$.. to help you to reduce your production costs, improve quality and maintain production schedules.

(Note the positive approach: to *reduce* ......, *improve*, ...... and *maintain*)

D. The object of the letter:

bring major benefits/be
of service

would welcome/would
be very happy to have

```
We believe that we can .....(7)..... to
your company and we .....(8)..... the
opportunity to discuss this with you.
```

E. Proposing action:

```
We are enclosing a resume of our
capabilities, also a list of our ..(9)..
..... We ..(10). to be in the United
Kingdom from early February through March
and would be available for any discussion.

(Note February through March is American
 English.  February to March is British
 English.)
```

key people/top
management

intend/propose

F. Closing the letter:

are interested/feel this is
of interest

contact us/let us know

```
If you .....(11)..... please .....(12).....
and we will arrange a meeting at your
convenience.
```

## B2 A 'soft sell' approach

Here is part of a direct mail letter with a more subtle selling approach than that given in **A2**.

Choose from the following phrases to fill in the gaps. Use each phrase once only.

highly specialised
engaged in
concern is with
in addition
to introduce our
company
all other energetic
companies
making our capabilities
known

```
Dear .......
We are writing ....(1)... Kane Kinetics Ltd.  We are ....(2)...
bio-mechanical engineering, research analysis and
consultation.  Our ....(3)... the study and evaluation of
human movement.
Like ....(4)... we maintain a research team.  This
provides insight into the relationship of men and
machines.
While our area of knowledge is ....(5)... its application
is wide.  Many of our major successes have been in
preventing industrial accidents.
....(6)... we are constantly searching for new sources
of business.  The search has taken us into the
international field, with emphasis on Europe.  We are
specially interested in ....(7)... in Switzerland.
Should this be of interest to you, we will be more
than happy to meet you to discuss your specific
requirements.


Very truly yours,
```

## B3 Standard reply to an enquiry

Here is the information an Italian company wishes to include in a standard letter to prospective customers who have made a general enquiry about their company policy regarding staff and equipment.

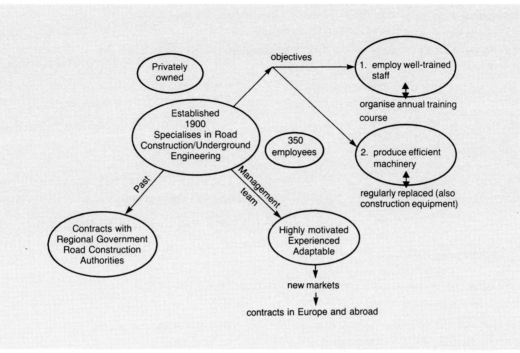

Complete the following letter by using the information which is contained in the diagram above.

Dear Sirs,

Thank you for your interest in our operation.

We would like to give you a brief introduction to our company.

It was founded in ..(1).. and developed to become one of the leading

..........(2)... in Italy.

Our main objectives have always been to .......(3)... and .......(4)..

As far as the first objective is concerned, we organise .......(5)..

and the second objective has been achieved by regularly .......(6)..

We employ .....(7).. In the past we have worked closely with .......(8)..

As our company is privately owned and the management team is .......(9)..,

we are now seeking .......(10)..

We enclose our company brochure which may answer some of your questions.

If you are interested, please ...

Write the final sentence to conclude this letter. Choose a phrase from
Column A and an ending from Column B to complete the letter.

| A | B |
|---|---|
| .................... do not hesitate to contact me. | Looking forward to hearing from you.<br>Yours sincerely, |
| .................... write to me at the above address. | I look forward to hearing from you in due course.<br>Yours faithfully, |
| .................... telephone me on this number. | I hope very much to be in contact with you again in the near future.<br>Yours sincerely, |

## C1   An American Brochure

It is important to be able to distinguish between fact and opinion when
reading a brochure, prospectus or press release.

Read this brochure carefully. As you read, decide which statements are
completely factual, and which statements are opinions.

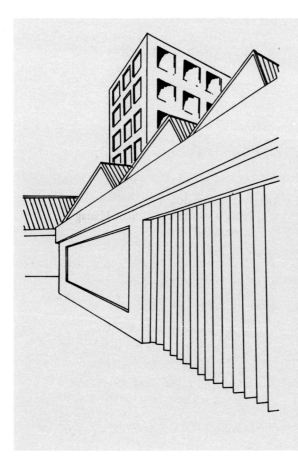

# We offer you an opportunity to participate

The Richard Baudin Corporation which has been
operating a successful textile-fiber processing plant
in Banbury, New Jersey, has transferred its manufacturing facility to Portugal in order to realise
maximum efficiency.

The move makes available for other use the
Company's well-located plant facilities as well as its
experienced and successful management and
engineering team.

The Company is interested in either a joint venture
with other responsible parties, in developing and
fabricating new products, or they will act as a
warehousing distributor for an established concern.

**Background history**

The Richard Baudin Corporation was founded in
1947 and has enjoyed a slow but steady growth
during this period.

The Company is keeping key personnel,
experienced in installation and maintenance of
mechanical equipment. Although the Company has
removed or is disposing of specialised production
machinery, some general purpose equipment has
been kept for future use.

## C2  Making a distinction between fact and opinion

(i)  Statements were made in the brochure in **C1** in order to make the proposal interesting and attractive.
What was *fact* and what was only an *opinion*?

The brochure says: 'a successful textile fiber ......'
Is that a fact or is it a subjective view?

Consider the following comments:
a.  Who can say the plant is 'well located'? Well located – for what?
b.  Is it only to 'realise maximum efficiency' that the plant has been transferred? Could there be another reason?
c.  Are the team really 'experienced' and 'successful'?
What evidence is there that they are so good?
d.  The brochure states that 'growth was slow but steady'. What is meant by that? How slow – how steady?

The above statements are all opinions. Refer to the brochure in **C1** and select the facts.
e.g. The Richard Baudin Corporation has operated a textile fiber processing plant in Banbury.

(ii)  Now complete the following sentences:

a.  The Company has transferred ....................
b.  ......... available ....................
c.  ......... interested in ....................
d.  ......... act as ....................
e.  ......... established in ....................
f.  ......... keeping ....................
g.  ......... removed ....................
h.  ......... disposing of ....................
i.  ......... been kept ....................

The brochure needs the opinions to make the text more interesting and to give it more impact.

## C3  Giving an opinion: expressing doubts and misgivings

(i)  A Company was interested in the Baudin Brochure. The Investment Manager was sent to New Jersey to inspect the property and to assess its potential. Here is an extract from the memo which accompanied the site plans. Read it carefully.

```
1.  We must take into consideration the fact that there
    is a lot of equipment surplus to our requirements
    when we negotiate the price.

2.  From past experience it would be advisable if we
    had more floor loading space.  At present it is
    barely adequate.

3.  While garage and workshop space is adequate,
    we must bear in mind that the structure is in poor
    condition.

4.  I have mixed feelings about the size of the
    property.  I would advise that we sold off part
    of the land.  Alternatively, we could consider
    the possibility of renting if we anticipate
    further expansion.

5.  The fact that the area is primarily devoted to
    tourism must be taken into account when
    considering labour availability.
```

(ii)  Expressing doubts
Note how the Investment Manager introduced his comments:
We must take into consideration ....................
From past experience it would be advisable .........
While ......... is adequate, we must bear in mind .........
I have mixed feelings about ....................
The fact that ......... must be taken into account.

This information must also be sent to the Company's Planning Consultant by telex. Re-write the five items above in telex form, using approximately half the number of words.

# UNIT 10

In this revision Unit you will find:
a press cutting, a postcard and letters and diagrams to stimulate a variety of letter writing exercises.

A. Exercises on making an enquiry, complaining and inviting
B. Exercises on composing a standard letter and report, note taking and summarising
C. Exercises on form-filling and writing letters of application and refusal

## A1   Exercise: Making an enquiry

Read the following extract from a press cutting about a recent demonstration flight of a helium filled airship. Note the comments in the margin.

What was unusual about the flight?

How much freight can be carried?

Who is supporting the proposed plan?

# HELIUM AIRSHIPS FLYING HIGH

Today the first fully operational helium filled airship was successfully flown in the South of England. It has a payload of over two tons and a cruising speed of 55 mph.

Within a few years the Company hopes to be producing more advanced airships which would carry 200 passengers or a 30 ton cargo up to 105 mph. The project is backed by Merchant Bankers, Insurance and Investment Companies.

An American Customs and Excise official, John Sonderson, was present at the demonstration flight. Here is the postcard he sent to his family.

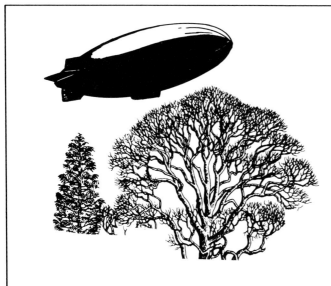

Saw maiden flight of this airship—most exciting, was v. impressed. Great potential for the future! We could do with a fleet of these for our job.

We leave tomorrow for Osaka. Back home on the 20th.

John

In what way has it potential.                    Had it flown before?


When John Sonderson returned to the USA he wrote to the manufacturers of the airship. Here is the reply he received.

Dear Mr Sonderson,

We were most interested to receive your letter of December 9th and to know that the Airship's performance on Friday far exceeded your expectations. As you are primarily interested in the use of this vehicle for anti-smuggling and Customs and Excise patrols, we would like you to meet our Technical Director to discuss your precise requirements.

The other developments in course of design include 30 ton and 70 ton capacity airships, though these will not come into production for three years. We appreciate that perhaps this is not of immediate interest, but you may wish to bear it in mind in your long term planning.

We look forward to hearing from you.
Yours sincerely,

Now write the original letter from Mr Sonderson to the manufacturers which prompted this reply. Refer to Unit 2 Section A for the layout and useful phrases.

After the introduction of your letter, explain the reason for your letter and your interest in airships, and make arrangements for future action.

### A2 Exercise: Letter of Enquiry

The freight manager of an East African company read an article about airships in a trade magazine. He is interested in the possibility of using airships to transport coffee from Kampala to Mombasa, a distance of 1600 kilometres. He anticipates a load would average 20 tons weekly.

Write the freight manager's letter of enquiry, including the following.
1. How you heard about airships.
2. Why you are interested.
3. Ask for background information – what are the advantages and disadvantages.

### B1 Exercise: Standard letter of reply

Compose a standard letter to reply to customers who have asked for general background information about airships. (See Unit 9 Section B). Thank the writer for his/her enquiry, and include the following points, which are in note form. In the left hand margin there are pairs of words which are similar in meaning. Insert the more appropriate word in the gap.

| | |
|---|---|
| require/take | - do not ..... runways |
| largely/highly | - ..... skilled maintenance personnel not required |
| take off/start up | - can .......... and land in remote areas |
| rate/ratio | - the load/fuel consumption ..... is excellent |
| compare/contrast | - freight rates would ..... favourably with Air Cargo rates. |
| congestion/constriction | - when transporting extra heavy equipment they would not cause road ..... |
| safe/secure | - ....., noiseless and pollution-free. |
| point-to-point/end-to-end | - can operate .......... therefore handling costs are reduced. |

End your letter by assuring the recipients that these advantages offer a considerable saving in cost to companies such as theirs.

Invite the recipients to give further details of their requirements.

## B2 Note-taking and summarising

\* You will require the notes you make in this section to complete the exercise in **B3**.

Read the following press cuttings carefully. Make notes of the really important information. Place your notes in the margin on the right. Use the headings which are given.

NOTES

Operating Costs

Initial Costs

as every freight operator knows, high cargo capacity is essential. In the airship, cargo space is 56% greater than in a jumbo jet. An estimate has been made of the operating costs per flying hour for a fifteen ton load; it is about one third of the conventional aircraft cost. At today's rate this would be in the region of $600 US. At present day prices the initial cost is approximately £1.4 M for an airship. This compares favourably with £1.5 M for a helicopter. A conventional jet is more expensive than a helicopter.

Speed?

Safety?

Noise?

Today, when speed is considered to be of paramount importance, the airship, with its low maximum speed, would be at a disadvantage. At 70 mph this compares unfavourably with both the helicopter at 140 mph and the jet at 600 mph. However, it has the added advantage that if something does go wrong with the engine, the airship would not crash to the ground. It would float down, or it could be towed away. When cruising, airships make less noise than a small helicopter and far less than a jet.

## B3   Making Comparisons

(i)  With all the information you have been given in **B2** complete the following table. Give each type of aircraft a performance rating of poor, fair or good.

|  | Helicopter | Jet | Airship |
|---|---|---|---|
| Operating Costs<br>Initial Cost<br>Speed<br>Safety<br>Noise<br>Endurance |  |  |  |

(ii)  Write sentences making comparisons between the types of aircraft. Use any of the following phrases or conjunctions:
   a.  Not only is the airship ......... to buy but it is also ......... to operate.
   b.  As well as being the ......... it is the ..........
   c.  Like ........., airships are much ......... than jets.
   d.  In addition, airships ...........
   e.  Although an ......... is slower, it is able to ..........
   f.  Both the ......... and the ......... are ...........

(iii)  Use the information you have already been given plus the comments below to write a brief composite report on airships. (See Unit 6 Sections A and B). Make recommendations how they could be used in *your* country.

the detecting and reporting of any illegal immigration and smuggling.

supplying oil rigs

air sea rescue

coastal patrol

Increasingly helicopters are being used for mine sweeping activities, but they are limited in this capacity as they must refuel every hour. The airship demonstrates advantages of high endurance.

hovering ability makes it ideal for surveying, laying pipe lines

airship has been designed as a multi-role vehicle with a large number of military and civilian applications.

the monitoring of all forms of environmental pollution and the early discovery of oil spills.

## C1   Exercise: Letter of application

Here is the official Permit to Fly which must be obtained before any trial flights can be made.

(i)  Read the entries carefully and use the information here to write the original letter of application for the permit.

**PERMIT TO FLY**

No. ZK – 1234

| NATIONALITY & REGISTRATION MARKS: | CONSTRUCTOR AND CONSTRUCTOR'S DESIGNATION OF AIRCRAFT: | AIRCRAFT SERIAL No.: |
|---|---|---|
| British G-ZABC | Norbrook Aviation Z - 10 | A/123 |
| CLASSIFICATION: | Airship - helium filled | CAPACITY: 300,000 cu. ft. |
| PURPOSES FOR WHICH THE AIRCRAFT MAY FLY: | Flight Testing | |
| FUEL: | 100 octane | |
| CREW: | Pilot, Navigator/Engineer | |
| OPERATOR OF THE AIRCRAFT: | NorbrAir | |
| ENGINE TYPE: | RZ 303 | |
| PROPELLER TYPE: | McHartzman - TVAM | |
| MAXIMUM NUMBER OF SEATS INCLUDING CREW: | 2 crew 16 passengers | |
| THE PERMIT IS VALID from | 24th September | |
| to | 23rd November | |

## Letter of application

(ii) Now write the original letter of application for a permit. All the
information you require is contained in the completed application form
in section (i).

Here are some phrases to guide you:

– we would like to apply for ......          – please note the following technical details ......
– the flight will be restricted to ......    – for flight testing the crew will consist of ......
– the relevant dates are ......              – the seating capacity ......

End your letter with a request to forward the permit as soon as possible.


## C2   A letter of refusal

A letter had also been sent by an international transport company to the
local Town Planning Committee asking for permission to establish a
terminal for airships and helicopters.

Here are extracts from the Committee's letter refusing permission. These
extracts are not in the correct sequence. Re-arrange them to form a coherent
letter. Your letter should not contain more than three paragraphs. (See Unit
2 Section D.)

```
Whilst there is an economic case
for such a project, our prime
responsibility is towards the local
population whose interests would be
adversely affected if permission
were granted.
```

```
Your recent application for an
airship and helicopter terminal
has been given every consideration,
but we regret that we are unable to
grant approval to the scheme as it
stands at present.
```

```
It is possible, that if you are
prepared to make certain
modifications to your original
proposal, and if you base your
calculation on not more than two
flights daily, the committee may
re-consider their decision.
```

```
We hope that you will appreciate
that we are determined to keep our
city in the forefront of
technological advance, but we are
equally determined to safeguard
the environment.
```

## C3　A letter of appeal

(i) *Assembling facts for an appeal to a higher authority.* The Operations
Manager decided to appeal against the Committee's decision. Here are
the notes he drew up in order to draft a letter to the Committee.

Study these notes, select the important facts to complete exercise (ii).

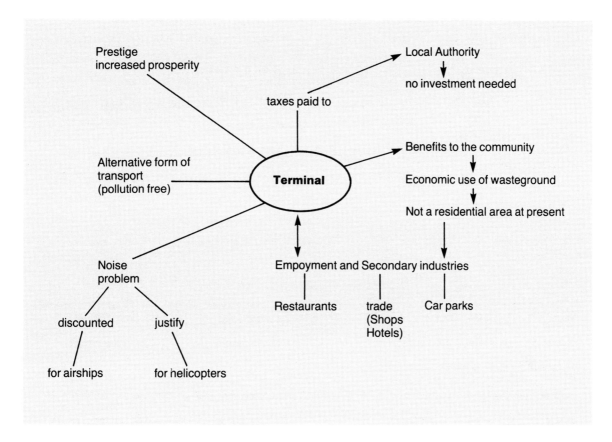

When you have studied the above notes, decide which facts you would use
to strengthen your appeal against the Committee's decision.

(ii) Refer to the letter of refusal in **C2** and the notes in **C3** (i) in order to complete the gaps in the following letter. Note the underlined phrases which introduce your case and strengthen your argument.

See **C2**

See **C3** (i)

> Dear Sir,
>
> Thank you for your letter of 22nd May.  I am afraid that I find it difficult to accept your reasoning. On the one hand you state that you are determined to ..... ..... and you agree that there is an economic ..... ..... for ..... ...... On the other hand you claim that the interests ..... .....
>
> It is evident that you have overlooked the benefits which ..... ..... will bring to ..... ...... Have you considered the following facts:
>
> ......................
>
> ......................
>
> ......................
>
> It may be argued that there would be a problem of ..... ..... but this fear has proved to be groundless. From the financial point of view ..... .....

Complete the letter by protesting that two flights a day would not be a viable proposition. Inform the committee that you intend to appeal to a higher authority, and ask them to forward all the necessary forms so that your appeal can be put in motion.

(iii) Give your own decision. Would you allow the terminal to be built?

# General notes to the Teacher

The material in this book gives full scope to the teacher who wishes to follow a humanistic approach. It enables the teacher to draw on the interests, knowledge and attitudes of the student.

Through a variety of activities the student will be personally involved in the situation presented in each unit.

To maintain the students' interest and allow for changes of pace any of the following techniques may be used.

## a. Brainstorming

Aim: To – elicit random ideas;
- prepare students for work on a given text;
- lead into a discussion or role play;
- pre-teach vocabulary;
- enable the student to contribute their personal ideas.

PROCEDURE

(i) Explain to the students that you want their ideas on a particular topic.
(ii) Introduce the topic orally or on the blackboard.
(iii) Place a time limit on the discussion at this stage and allow the students to pour out their associated ideas at random. Accept words or phrases and do not question what is offered. Make any grammatical correction if necessary without comment.
(iv) When you feel they have exhausted the topic, encourage individual students to clarify words or phrases which may be new to other students. Check pronunciation. Make a note of any grammar difficulties.
(v) The ideas generated may spark off a spontaneous discussion. Let it flow. Or you may wish to introduce the next stage of the lesson.

The students will now be well prepared to focus on the task in store. This may be a listening comprehension or a reading or writing exercise.

## b. Segmented texts

Aim: To – lighten the reading load;
- encourage student talking time;
- develop group dynamics;
- change the pace of a lesson;
- get students up from their seats;
- deal with mixed ability students.

PROCEDURE

(i) If the class is large, divide it into convenient smaller groups. For example, 16 students can be divided into four groups of four students or, if it is more convenient, two groups of eight.
(ii) You require a photocopy of the text for each group. Before you go into the class cut up each photocopy into sections. Each section should finish at the end of a sentence.

Distribute one section to each student (out of sequence). The stronger students can be given a more demanding section of text than that given to the weaker students.
(iii) Each student studies his/her section without showing the written text to the other students. Students read aloud or tell their group (according to their capabilities) what is written on their section.
(iv) Teacher 'hovers' and checks any vocabulary difficulties. Be unobtrusive at this stage. Whisper corrections into the students' ear if necessary. Avoid eye contact with the students.
(v) Students now discuss and arrange the text in its original sequence. Keep well out of the way and allow the students to work things out for themselves.

## c. Mirror questions (Self to self)

Aim: To – check vocabulary and comprehension;
– form questions;
– practice skim reading;
– lead into a discussion arising from the text;
– give practice in forming questions.

The question posed may range from simple 'Can you . . .?' 'Do you . . .?' producing a 'yes/no' response, or the 'wh' type which demand fuller detail. The complexity of the structures depends on the aim of the lesson and the students' ability.

## PROCEDURE

(i) Students are given a text of approximately 250 words to read silently.
(ii) Students prepare and write down a given number of questions on the text they have just read which they would be prepared to answer.
(iii) Teacher 'hovers', checks the written questions, and helps with correction.
(iv) Students pair off.
(v) Students exchange the paper on which they have written their questions.
(vi) A asks B B's questions. B answers from memory without referring to the text.
(vii) A checks B's answer by referring to the text if necessary.
(viii) Vice versa. B asks A A's questions.

It is interesting for the students to compare the types of question used.
An alternative is to
(i) Pair the students at the beginning of the exercise.
(ii) Give each student in the pair a different text to read.
(iii) Students write their questions.
(iv) Exchange their questions and texts.
(v) Student A asks A's questions, and is obliged to skim read A's text in order to check the answers.

## d. Dictogloss

Aim: To – give practice in prediction, listening and note taking. It is a useful revision exercise and a self correction technique. It also provides a useful lead-in to a role play.

## PROCEDURE

(i) Choose a short text to read (between 50–100 words). The text may include names, facts, and figures.
(ii) Write a headline on the blackboard connected with the text to be read. Invite the students to speculate about the heading, and create a possible story behind the heading.
(iii) Warn the students they will hear the passage read once only.
(iv) Read the passage at a little slower than normal speed.
(v) Invite the students to write notes as you dictate.
(vi) Students then work individually and re-write the passage in their own words but reflecting the content. Give the students plenty of time.)
(vii) Students form pairs. They compare their texts and compose a joint version. One acts as secretary, the other dictates as slowly as necessary. Encourage students to correct each other.

This can be extended by the students writing four or five questions they would like to ask each character who featured in the text. This then leads naturally into a role-play

(viii) Alternatively, choose a student's text to write on the blackboard. Deal with any specific grammar points which may emerge.
(ix) Hand out the original text, for students to compare with their own version.

### e. Role play or improvisation

Aim: To – vary the pace of a lesson;
- encourage the use of language just learnt by transferring the written word to the spoken word;
- encourage an awareness of register;
- liven up the students by pair or group work;
- give practice in summarising a text.

### PROCEDURE

(i) Choose material involving a variety of emotions or incidents, not a descriptive passage.

(ii) Give students text(s) in question.

(iii) In pairs, or small groups students summarise the situation.

(iv) Hand out a card to each pair or group on which you have written the character and the location of the scene you want them to work on.

e.g. husband to wife at home; wife to husband at a formal dinner; woman to employer at a board meeting; man to friend over a casual drink.

(v) The students can re-form pairs or stay as they were in (iii) and between them they work out a dialogue.

(vi) Students act out their dialogues and the rest of the class decide just what their relationship is and where the scene is taking place, or the students could record their dialogues to play to another pair.

Throughout the teacher can 'hover', check grammar, pronunciation, and guide the student to the appropriate register. A word of warning: discourage the students from reading their script. It may be non-effective if the students outline the shape of the exchange, for example

. .$\overset{A}{.}$. thanks . $\overset{B}{.}$.;
. .$\overset{B}{.}$. enquires . . .;
. . . checks and denies knowledge of . . .;
. . . reminds . . .;
. . . responds and ends . . .

### FOLLOW UP:

Different ways of performing the same function can be noted and fully practised.

### f. Group decision making

Aim: To – use transactional language, agreeing, disagreeing, offering alternatives;
- practice specific tenses – past, future or modals, or sequencing vocabulary;
- improve group dynamics;
- practice all four skills;
- lead into report writing, summarising or role playing.

### PROCEDURE

(i) Select an activity with a logical sequence of events, for example buying a house, extending a house or factory, opening a new shop.

(ii) List the different events which will have to take place. For example if you decide on buying a house,
- place an advertisement in a paper;
- decide which area/town you are going to move to;
- get a survey done;
- sell your house;
- buy furniture;
- look at new houses;
- install central heating.

(iii) Compose a handout for your students and explain that these were activities either done last year (if you wish the past tense to be practised) or which have to be done next year if you wish your students to practice modals. Do not place the events in the correct sequence.

(iv) Make a photocopy for each group of students and check vocabulary. At this stage you may wish to discuss each stage. For example, what is involved in getting a survey done, what sort of advertisement. Get the students to write the advertisement, choose the furniture, discuss what is the best form of central heating, etc., etc.

(v) In groups the students work out the logical sequence of events. There must be a consensus of opinion to work out the critical path analysis and draw up a diagram of their findings.

(vi) Students are asked to write five sentences explaining their course of action. Prompts may be given to elicit

the required structure, e.g.

| | | |
|---|---|---|
| Having done . . . | you | should |
| After . . . ing . . . | | must |
| Before . . . ing . . . | | ought to |
| | or | |
| First of all we . . . | | |
| Then we . . . | | |
| Eventually . . . | | |
| Finally . . . | | |
| etc. | | |

FOLLOW UP:

A summary or report of their findings can be written for homework. As the students to prepare a similar list of events which you could use with a lower class.

# KEY

UNIT 1

**A1  An informal letter**
1/c; 2/f; 3/d; 4/b; 5/e; 6/a.

**B2  Establishing the tone of a letter**
1 – to inform; 2 – to apologise; 3 – to threaten; 4 – to sympathise.

**B3  Exercises in opening and ending your letter**
a/(iii) – to invite; b/(i) – to complain; c/(v) – to give an ultimatum; d/(ii), – to congratulate; e/(iv) – to thank.

**C2  Phrasal verbs**
look through it/review; weigh it up/evaluate; work out/determine; tie up/finalise; fix up/negotiate; sort out/settle; talk over/discuss; look over/inspect.
Note that the phrasal verbs do not necessarily carry exactly the same implications as their one-word equivalents. For further information, consult a good recent dictionary of phrasal verbs.

**C3  File memos**
1/on; 2/in; 3/by; 4/at; 5/of; 6/with; 7/of; 8/over; 9/for; 10/in.

**D3  Telexes**
1/investigate; 2/company's; 3/background; 4/assure; 5/will; 6/treated.

**D4** Reply to Mr. Ioannou from his friend in Milan *(Specimen answer)*

Dear Mr Ioannou,
Thank you for your telex of 18th August concerning the possible takeover of Albani.

As far as I can see, it is highly unlikely that it is in any immediate danger of being taken over. The main reason why, at present, there is no need for concern, is that the family who own the company wish to maintain control. I can assure you that, to judge from the discreet enquiries I have made, they are not short of capital, and I cannot see any reason why you should not continue trading with them. However, if I hear anything to the contrary I will, of course, contact you.

NB: (i) 'to take over' but 'a takeover'.
(ii) At the start of the letter the company is referred to in the singular: 'it'. By the end of the letter, having mentioned that the company is owned by a group of people, the writer changes it to the plural: 'them'.

UNIT 2

**A3  Booking accommodation**
Dear Sir,
Following my phone call this morning I am writing to confirm that we wish to book a conference room from 11.00 on August 18th to

16.00 on August 26th for our annual sales conference.

Just to remind you, we require a large room, as 30 people will be attending the conference. Also, could you please ensure that there is an electric socket near the top table for our overhead projector. (We would like to use your screen.)

I forgot to talk in detail about catering. Could you please confirm that buffet facilities will be available. We expect to break for lunch about 12.30 each day.

## B1 Active and passive voice
1. You have not paid your bill.
2. I will pick him up at 07.00.
3. The board did not show any immediate interest.
iv. No record of this account can be found.
5. We will have to make salary cuts and shorten holidays.
vi. A mistake has been made and a loss incurred. (NB: there is no need to repeat 'has been' in 'has been incurred'.)
7. You have overdrawn your account to the extent of £187. We have made arrangements to forward a statement to you so you can check your exact position

## B2 Vocabulary building
Most adjectives can be used with more than one noun, but note particularly the following combinations.

Suitable partner (e.g. 'we are looking for a suitable partner to join us in a new venture which . . .'); excellent facilities (e.g. 'our factory has excellent facilities for staff including a cafeteria, car park and games room.'); favourable terms (e.g. 'favourable terms for the new agency agreement have now been agreed by both sides.); important manufacturer (e.g. 'X is an important manufacturer of domestic appliances, having 53% of the home market.') (NB: you can not say 'an important turnover' – use 'large' instead.); competitive prices (e.g. 'They have reduced their profit margin and are now offering competitive prices which we will find hard to beat.'); industrial know how (e.g. 'Having worked in the field of shipbuilding for many years they have acquired a great deal of industrial knowhow which would be useful for us.'); careful consideration (e.g. 'We have all thought about and talked over your proposition, but despite careful consideration we regret we are unable to accept it.'); technical facilities (e.g. 'The new plant has excellent technical facilities including

research laboratories and an automated production line.')

## B3 Describing a location
Kenyan safari park/conservation; Norwegian hotel/tourism; Scottish sports complex/leisure and recreation (NB: Scotch whisky, Scots people); Japanese steel factory/heavy industry; Spanish art gallery/cultural activities; Turkish warehouse/general industrial use; Canadian nature park/preservation.

## C2 Supplying information
2. At present the market is supplied only by low-quality imports at local current prices. As a result, the demand for high-quality goods is not high.
3. Despite the fact that the local labour force was unskilled, we required a number of skilled operators to be trained by the end of the first year.
4. At present facilities are limited. Nevertheless, plans have been made to remedy the situation.
5. There are generous tax incentives for new industries. In fact, there is a 40% tariff on all imports.
6. We now have excellent road and rail services as well as river transport to major ports.
7. A power station opened last year. Consequently, we have more power than expected, as well as an adequate water supply.

## D2 Letters of refusal: sample replies
Situation 1
Thank you for your letter of 18th February, and for the interest you show in our products. We regret that we are unable to offer you an exclusive agency for whole region, as you suggest. The main reason for this is that the Torin company have acted as our representatives in that area for many years, and we are not currently thinking of altering the arrangement.

However, we would consider offering you a non-exclusive sub-agency for your town, for a one-year trial period. Alternatively, you may prefer Torin to supply you directly. I am sure they would offer very favourable terms for bulk purchase, and I am therefore copying this letter to their Managing Director, Mr Jones.

Situation 2
Thank you for your letter of 2nd August. Unfortunately, we are unable to grant the loan you require, according to the information you supplied, you still have insufficient collateral in this country.

May we suggest instead a third party

guarantee? We can assure you that we could then offer you a loan on very favourable terms.

Situation 3

Many thanks indeed for your letter. I had actually been meaning to get in touch about your order, to remind you that we have already given you an extension of 60 days beyond normal, and, as you have several orders due for delivery in the near future, we would appreciate payment as soon as possible. In the circumstances I'm sure you will appreciate that we could not possibly give a second extension of credit. One way of getting round this might be this. How about paying by Bill of Exchange, accepted 120 days from invoice – interest to be paid by you? I look forward to hearing from you.

# UNIT 3

## A1 Confirmation of an order
(i) Letter to Lanificio Bonardi
1. This is to confirm . . . 2. We must point out that . . . 3. We would like your assurance that . . . 4. at the latest. 5. May we remind you to . . . 6. Could you please check . . . 7. to avoid a recurrence. 8. the date of invoice.
(ii) b. 1. Please specify despatch date, giving details of method of shipment.
2. Please indicate the completion date, bearing in mind the factory holiday.
3. Please quote your most favourable terms, not forgetting our loyalty discount.
(iii) a. They insisted there should be no corrosion.
b. It is vital that there is no deterioration in the quality of the drug.
c. It is important that packing will protect against breakage and theft.
(NB: 'Packing' but 'a package'.)

## A3 Telex requesting action
a. SHIPPER INFORMS US DOCUMENTS TO CLEAR GOODS ARE MISSING.
b. IMPERATIVE YOU LOCATE THEM IMMEDIATELY.
c. POST DOCUMENTS EXPRESS TO DUNCAN AND GRANT, SHIPPERS, IF YOU FIND THEM.
d. DEMURRAGE AND CONSEQUENTIAL LOSS WILL BE CHARGED TO YOU.

## B1 (iii) Letter of apology (sample)
We are sorry to tell you that we may not be able to meet our delivery date for your order. What happened was that the shipping documents were delayed for certification, and, though your materials had arrived, our shippers were unable to clear them.

We shall do everything possible to minimise the delay, and have arranged to start production in a few days.

Once again, we apologise for the delay, and assure you the order will be in Jersey early in October.

## B2 (ii)
1. threatening, 25th Sept., probably, may well.
2. now arrived, must, this week.
3. must.

## B3 Telex advising delivery
1. DESPATCHING ALL TEN CASES SEPTEMBER 20.
2. SENDING BY SS MARIANA SAILING SOUTHAMPTON SEPTEMBER 22.
3. AIRMAILING ALL DOCUMENTS, INVOICES TO HOTEL SAME DAY.
4. INSURING SHIPMENT CIF VALUE PLUS 10 PERCENT.
(NB: CIF = Cost Insurance and Freight. FOB = Free On Board.)

## C1 An insurance claim
(ii) a. Hotel interiors; b. Brampton Hospital; c. 4 chairs didn't arrive; d. £560; e. £560; f. yes; g. yes; h. 4 chairs missing.

## C2 Questions: making enquiries
d/1; f/2; c/3; a/4; b/5; h/6; e/7; i/8; g/9.

## C3 A statement
1. reported; 2. questioned; 3. denied; 4. insisted; 5. maintained; 6. protested.

# UNIT 4

## A2 An informal letter of congratulation
I was very glad to hear about your recent appointment. I know how hard you have worked, and you certainly deserve it. It is a great pity we can't get together soon. I'm going to the States for two weeks but I'll give you a ring when I get back. Meanwhile, all the very best for the future.

## C1
Company B has been a supplier for five years and has supplied goods on 60 days' credit to a limit of £10 000. They report that the hotel is experiencing temporary cash flow problems.

Company C has been a supplier for two years and supplied goods on 90 days' credit to a limit of £3000. However, recently the hotel exceeded these terms and supplies had to be stopped.
(NB: 'Supplied goods' not 'has supplied goods' since they are no longer doing so.)
Company D has only been a supplier for nine months. It supplied goods on 30 days' credit up to a limit of £2000. They report that the hotel normally pays after a second reminder.

## C2  Pressing for payment
1. despite; 2. settled; 3. to date; 4. originally; 5. specially; 6. understanding; 7. breakdown; 8. arrange; 9. in full; 10. reason; 11. touch.

## UNIT 5

### A1  Summary of Professor Marsh's letter to Dr Adelby
After referring to her lecture and reminding her of their conversation, Marsh invited Adelby to join his Brunei expedition, outlining its aims and warning it was not well paid. He explained that the next step was an agreement in principle and asked when she would next be in Britain.

### B3  Informal acceptance
1. to confirm; 2. Many thanks; 3. as though; 4. sort out; 5. fairly; 6. contact; 7. get in; 8. let me.

### C2  Altering arrangements
a. To your bank manager
I sincerely regret that I shall be unable to keep our appointment on Tuesday at 4 pm, when we were due to discuss my overdraft. I attempted to contact you on the telephone but was unable to, and now have to attend an unexpected Board meeting that afternoon. Would it be possible to arrange another time? Specifically, would 2 pm the same day be convenient for you?
Yours sincerely,
b. To a colleague
I'm sorry, but I will be unable to keep our lunch date at 12.45 next Friday. I tried to get hold of you on the telephone, but wasn't able to – and have just learnt that I've got to go to Paris next Thursday for a meeting. Can we fix up another time? Would 12.30 on the following Monday be possible?
Best wishes,

### D2  Choosing the correct preposition
Financed by; consists of; authorised by (someone) to (do something); in (a subject) at (a college or university); specialises in; works for (a firm, etc) with (colleagues) at (place); on (a topic), about (a topic); interest in (people or subjects); by (an authority) for (the people seeking permission) to (do something); by coincidence; to (doing something).

## UNIT 6

### A1  NOTE TAKING
1. To begin with; 2. a while; 3. initially; 4. later; 5. subsequently; 6. after which; 7. previously; 8. due course; 9. first; 10. later; 11. After; 12. finally.

### A2
Before Mr and Mrs Mitchell's first visit to the counsellor, Mrs Mitchell had been attacked and hit by her husband. This had happened during a violent argument which had originally begun when their son asked to be allowed to borrow their car. The attack was seen by their son, Anthony. Later that day, Anthony was charged with stealing goods from a shop.
It is hoped that the following facts will be thought about when Mr Anthony Mitchell comes before the court.
(NB: In this particular case, the more formal style is probably more appropriate. But there are many cases in which an over-formal style will give the wrong impression.)

### A3  Expanding notes
Mr Mitchell is increasingly in danger of losing his job.
Mr Mitchell is increasingly influenced by friends.

### B2  Formal and informal language
a. I am now confident that if Anthony is permitted to continue his studies he will achieve high academic standards.
b. I wish to stress that Anthony's very difficult family circumstances should be taken into account when his case comes up for review.

### B3  Making recommendations (suggested version)
Having taken into consideration the facts which led up to the charge of shoplifting, we hope you will be as sympathetic as possible in your judgement. We think that Anthony should be given the chance to resit his examinations and

continue his studies. It would be much
appreciated if Anthony could be discharged and
allowed to make a new start.
(NB: Note how this includes a mixture of formal
   and less formal words.)

## C1 Talking about statistics

According to the graph above, convictions for
stealing cars have almost halved in the past 10
years. The figure was at its lowest seven years ago,
but after the introduction of lighter penalties the
downward trend was halted, and the number of
thefts rose steadily from around 20 000 to 28 000.
This rise reflects an annual increase of over 6%.

## C2 Language for interpreting a graph

1. fluctuated; 2. rose gradually; 3. rise;
4. gradual fall; 5. sharp recovery; 6. erratic;
7. dramatic fall, when prices took a plunge and
in fact declined to their lowest that year;
8. trough; 9. steady increase; 10. levelled off;
11. plateau; 12. leapt upwards; 13. peak.

## UNIT 7

## A1 A letter of complaint
   a. After repeated unsuccessful attempts to put
      forward new ideas, he resigned.
   b. Having left the car at the depot, I caught the
      plane to Copenhagen.
   c. Having spoken to the company secretary I
      decided to write to you.

## A2 Polite complaint and strong accusation
   (i) a. I was delayed.
       b. I was assured that everything was alright.
       c. I was given the wrong car.
       d. A mistake was made.
       e. I have been caused a lot of frustration.
   (ii) 1/c; 2/f; 3/4; 4/b; 5/a; 6/g; 7/e.

## A3 Letter of complaint
   (i) 1. On inspection; 2. original;
       3. emphasise; 4. particular; 5. be grateful;
       6. could; 7. replacement.
   (ii) 1. persuaded; 2. purchase; 3. trouble;
        4. under guarantee; 5. adjustment; 6. still;
        7. defective; 8. prepared; 9. appreciate.

## B2 Formal and informal language
   a. We are sorry, but we are unable to extend
      your credit.
   b. Thank you for asking me to speak to your
      members. I am sorry that I have to turn down
      the invitation, but . . ..
   c. I would personally suggest that you get in
      touch with our local representative.

## B3 Responding to letters of complaint
   (i) 1. sincere; 2. suggest; 3. either; 4. or;
       5. stands; 6. allowance; 7. regret;
       8. production.
   (ii) 1. very sorry to hear; 2. have arranged for;
        3. contact you; 4. suit your convenience;
        5. sent to you; 6. are certain; 7. find it
        satisfactory; 8. apologise sincerely.

## D1 Letters of apology and settlement
   a. and b.: Specimen reply using both more and
   less formal phrases.
   1. most concerned; 2. consideration; 3. accept
   our apologies; 4. suddenly taken ill;
   5. accidentally; 6. re-considering the
   circumstances; 7. position; 8. unreasonable;
   9. stick to; 10. we are happy to enclose;
   11. negligently; 12. unsafe; 13. defective;
   14. assurance; 15. give us the chance.

## UNIT 8

## A1 Specimen rewording of grant advertisement
The Sara Jensen memorial award offers grants to
women already successfully established in their
own career to use their skills in a different field
overseas for one year. Candidates, who must
offer reasons for eligibility, will select their own
project (subject to approval) and give details of
how they would spend the grant. Contact: Anne
Ridley.

## A3 Job requirements: sample advertisements
   (i) We are looking for a clerk to join our large
       furniture store. Book-keeping and accounts
       are essential, and experience with
       computerised ledger systems would be an
       advantage. If you have an orderly and
       methodical mind and are capable of
       consistent accurate work, why not write for
       an application form?

       (N.B. Note the fairly informal style, addressing
           applicants in the second person.)

   (ii) Our client is a small electronics firm. Small
        at present, but not for long, as they are
        rapidly breaking into the American market.
        They therefore wish to make the key
        appointment of Export Manager. The
        successful applicant, who should have at
        least five years experience at equivalent

level, will be expected to spearhead the company's export drive.

(N.B. Note the use of the third person. The advert has been placed by a recruitment agency, asked by the firm to find a suitable person. The language in these adverts is almost invariably optimistic – no doubts about the company's growth. Applicants are left in no doubt that if they don't make the grade, they're out! The abbreviation £20K is common but should not be used.)

(iii) The company   A medium sized industrial company.
The post   Medical advisor, able to encourage on positive staff attitude to health and safety at work.
The challenge   Due to the introduction of a new process involving the use of asbestos, the postholder must be fully aware of all relevant legislation.

(N.B. Both these jobs carry the implication that there are problems involved. Phrases like 'the company was forced to revise downwards its employee requirements' are just a way of saying that it sacked a large part of its work force. In the second advert, why is there a mention of asbestos legislation?)

## C4  Language for writing a reference
(i) Wanjuki was an effective leader.
(ii) Wanjuki was an effective office administrator.
(iii) Wanjuki was an effective designer.
(iv) Wanjuki was an effective manager.

## UNIT 9

## A3  Modifying a standard letter
(ii)
a. and b.  Paragraph 2 in letter is A2.
We are not brokers but an international consulting firm of professional executives who have helped their clients on many occasions to expand their operations in the States. We work full time for clients . . ..

c.  Paragraph 4 in letter is A2.
If this idea interests you, we can prepare a general proposal, which would describe in detail how the program works, with no obligation on your part whatsoever. When you have read . . . .

## B1  Standard paragraphs
The correct order of paragraphs is: C, B, A, D, E, F.

## B2  A 'soft-sell' approach
1. to introduce our company;  2. engaged in;
3. concern is with;  4. all other energetic companies;  5. highly specialised;  6. in addition;  7. making our capabilities known.

## B3  Standard reply to an enquiry
1. 1900;  2. road construction and underground engineering;  3. employ well-trained staff;
4. produce efficient machinery;  5. an annual training course;  6. replacing equipment and construction machinery;  7. 350 employees;
8. regional road construction authorities;
9. adaptable and highly motivated;  10. new markets in Europe and further afield.
If you are interested, please write to me at the above address. I hope very much to be in contact with you again in the near future. Yours sincerely, . . . .

## C2  Making a distinction between fact and opinion
(ii) a.  The company has transferred its manufacturing facility to Portugal.
b.  The move makes available its US plant facilities.
c.  The company is interested in a joint venture.
d.  Or, it may act as a warehousing distribution for an established concern.
e.  The company was established in 1947.
f.  The company is keeping key personnel.
g.  The company has removed specialised production machinery.
h.  Some general purpose machinery has been kept.

## C3  (ii) Suggested telex
MUCH SURPLUS EQUIPMENT WHICH SHOULD NOT BE INCLUDED IN PRICE. FLOOR LOADING SPACE INADEQUATE. STRUCTURE OF GARAGE AND WORKSHOP POOR THOUGH SPACE ADEQUATE. CONSIDER SELLING PART OF LAND, OR RENTING IF EXPANSION POSSIBLE. TOURIST AREA, WHICH MAY AFFECT LABOUR AVAILABILITY.

**A2** Specimen letter of enquiry

I am Freight Manager with an East African company. One of our activities is transporting coffee from Kampala to Mombasa. I was interested to read in our trade magazine the recent article about airships, as the payload of your airship would seem to correspond to our requirements. I would be grateful if you could send me some background information on airships, including the disadvantages as well as advantages. You may like to know that we already lease two cargo aircraft.

**B1** Specimen letter of reply (*extract*)

Thank you for your letter of (date) concerning our airships. The enclosed brochure gives further details, but you may like to consider the following advantages of airships over heavier than air machines. They do not require runways and highly skilled maintenance personnel, and are very versatile, being able to take off and land in remote areas.

Economy in terms of load/fuel consumption ratio is excellent, with the result that freight rates would compare favourably with air cargo rates, with the added attraction that they can operate point-to-point, therefore reducing handling costs.

Turning to other factors, airships are safe, noiseless and pollution free, and of course when transporting extra heavy equipment they would not cause road congestion.

We are sure that all these factors together would offer your company a considerable all-round saving in cost, and would be delighted to help you further if you could give us more details of your requirements.

**B3  Making comparisons**

(ii) a.  Not only is the airship the least expensive to buy, it is also the cheapest to operate.

b.  As well as being the safest, it is the quietest.

c.  Like helicopters, airships are much slower than jets.

d.  In addition, airships make less noise than either helicopters or jets.

e.  Although an airship is not as fast, it is able to stay in the air longer.

f   Both the helicopter and the airship are able to fly much slower than jets.

**C1** (ii) Specimen letter of application

We would like to apply for a permit to fly for helium-filled airship G-ZABC, serial no. A/123. This is a Z-10 built by Norbrook Aviation and operated by NorbrAir. The flights will be restricted to flight testing, between 24th September and 23rd November inclusive.

Please note the following technical details. Engine type – R2 303; Propellor type – McHartzmann-TVAM; Fuel – 100 octane; Capacity (helium) – 300 000 cubic feet.

Though for normal purposes the airship can also carry 16 passengers, for flight testing the crew will be restricted to the usual pilot and navigator/engineer.

We would be grateful if you could forward the permit as soon as possible as we are anxious to begin trials.

**C3  (ii)  Letter of refusal**

Thank you for your letter of 22nd May. I am afraid I find it difficult to accept your reasoning. On the one hand you state you are determined to keep this city in the foreground of technological advance, and you agree there is an economic case for such a project. On the other hand you claim that the interests of the local population are your prime responsibility.

It is evident that you have overlooked the benefits which economic use of a piece of waste ground will bring to the community. Have you considered the following facts? The area is currently non-residential. Employment will be created by restaurants and similar establishments, trade will be generated – obviously of benefit to local shops and hotels, and secondary industries such as car parks may well be established in due course. It may be argued that there would be a problem of noise and pollution but this fear has proved to be groundless. From the financial point of view, no investment will be required of the Local Authority, which will in turn benefit from taxes generated by the development.

The two flights a day you propose to allow us would not be a viable economic proposition, and so I have no option other than to appeal to a higher authority. I would therefore be grateful if you could forward all the necessary forms so we can put the appeal in motion.